LIFE CHANGING PRINCIPLES
FOR VICTORIOUS LIVING

*Keys to Unlock Your
New Life in Christ*

DR. SHAUN MARLER

Life Changing Principles for Victorious Living
by Dr. Shaun Marler

Published by:
World Harvest Ministries, PO Box 90, Bald Hills, Qld, 4036, Australia
www.whm.org.au

This book or parts thereof may not be reproduced in any form, stored in a retrieval system, or transmitted in any form, by any means - electronic, mechanical, photocopy, recording or otherwise - without prior written permission of the author or publisher, except as provided by Australian copyright law.

All scriptural references are taken from the King James Bible unless otherwise stated.

Cover Design by Cherise Durham & Sarah Freeman
Front Cover Picture: Fotohunter/Shutterstock.com
Back Cover Picture: Romolo Tavani/Shutterstock.com

Copyright © Shaun Marler 1987

First Published May 2020

ISBN: 978-0-6485897-0-9

THIS BOOK IS DEDICATED TO
THE EXTENSION OF THE KINGDOM OF GOD.

I would like to dedicate this book to the new believer in Christ and those who just want to learn more.

You have just begun an exciting journey, that will give you great joy and lead you to the most amazing places.

The number one key to success in life is to, Seek First the Kingdom of God and His Righteousness. God promises that when we do this, He will add to our lives everything we need. Then we will enjoy a rich and full life in His blessings, not having to care about what tomorrow may bring.

As you grow in your faith, I pray the revelation of God's word, contained in the teachings found in this book will inspire and encourage you to reach for God's best in life!

Much love in Jesus,

Ps. Shaun Marler

Foreword

I was honored to be asked to introduce people to this wonderful book, *"Life Changing Principles For Victorious Living"* written by Pastor Shaun Marler, Senior Pastor and co-founder with his wife Kerrie, of World Harvest Ministries, based in Queensland, Australia.

Pastor Shaun has been very instrumental in spreading the message of God's Word and The Blessing to the people in Australia and other parts of the world. He has a Pastor's heart for God's people and has dedicated his life to telling the world about the salvation and goodness of our wonderful Lord and Savior, Jesus.

I found this book to be a fantastic introduction and description of the Spirit Filled Life, which will also be very informative to mature believers. It is a great place to start your study of God's Word. It is full of information on the important topics in the bible and is easy to read and understand, even for the new believers.

I would have loved to have had this book available to me after I received Jesus as my Savior. It took me many years to learn what the reader will learn in only a few, short, enjoyable hours with this amazing book. This book would also be excellent for Bible Study and Home Fellowships groups. It can also be used as a reference book.

Take your time, as you read through this book, as there is so much valuable information and insight in these pages. You are going to acquire an understanding of the principles of the Spirit Filled Life, which most Born Again Believers do not have. You will learn what a wonderful God we serve, a God who loves us with a love that cannot be described.

Pastor Shaun not only reveals God's will and promises in this book, but tells readers how to receive them for themselves in order to live a healthy, happy and abundant life.

For new Believers, this book is a great place to start your study of God's Word. For people who have had a long relationship with Jesus, you will be amazed by how much you will learn and grow in faith and grace as a result of reading this book.

This book should be read over and over and it is my prayer that God will open your heart and help you receive these words into your heart.

May God Bless You Abundantly,

Pastor Jim Kibler
Author and Senior Pastor of Life Church, Melbourne, Florida.

I have known Pastor Shaun Marler for some years now and have had the pleasure of ministering at his church World Harvest Ministries in Brisbane, Australia.

I believe that Pastor Shaun has covered the basic principles of the Christian Faith in a clear and easily understood manner.

This book will be a most valuable asset for both new believers and those more mature in the Faith.

I have no hesitation in recommending this book to you.

Yours,

Dr Jerry Savelle
Noted author, evangelist, pastor and teacher.
International headquarters in Crowley, Texas.

It has been my great pleasure to read Pastor Shaun Marler's timely book. I have known Shaun and Kerrie for many years and hold them in high esteem. Shaun is well experienced to write such an informative book as this, he is a successful pastor, evangelist and teacher.

In his book, Shaun covers what Salvation entails - healing, protection, provision etc, as well as such important matters as End Times and Communion. The other thing I like is the question and answer section at the end of every chapter.

I highly recommend Shaun's book and believe it will prove a valuable resource to new believers, as well as Christians who need to know more about these very important topics.

Dr Col Stringer
Author of 20 books including '800 Horsemen' and noted speaker.

Acknowledgements

It was over thirty years ago that Dr. Steve Ryder asked me to compile a list of teachings to help the thousands of converts that were led to the Lord in Czechoslovakia, during his great Reach Out for Christ Healing Crusades.

Drawing from many sources and my own study of God's Word, I compiled these powerful and life changing principles.

For more than thirty years they have blessed thousands that have read and studied them. I know they will now be life changing for you, as you also study and apply these principles to your life.

A big thank-you to all the great men and women of faith that have personally sown into my life and have helped me produce this valuable work.

THANK YOU

To everyone who has helped me prepare this book, I extend my gratitude and special thanks: to Cherise Durham and Sarah Freeman for helping me bring this book to completion, and also to my wonderful wife Kerrie, for her support and constant prayers for this ministry and many contributions to and editing this work.

Contents

Introduction 15

Chapter One BORN AGAIN - WHAT DOES IT MEAN? 19

Chapter Two LORDSHIP OF JESUS 33

Chapter Three WATER BAPTISM 39

Chapter Four BAPTISM OF THE SPIRIT 45

Chapter Five TONGUES 53

Chapter Six YOU ARE THE RIGHTEOUSNESS OF GOD IN CHRIST ... 61

Chapter Seven PRAYER 69

Chapter Eight GOD'S WORD MUST BE CONFESSED 79

Chapter Nine CONFESSIONS FOR VICTORY 89

Chapter Ten FAITH 95

Chapter Eleven ABUNDANT VICTORIOUS LIFE 103

Chapter Twelve HEALING... 115

Chapter Thirteen NINE STEPS TO DIVINE HEALING 127

Chapter Fourteen LAYING ON OF HANDS 135

Chapter Fifteen GIVING AND RECEIVING 155

Chapter Sixteen THE IMPORTANCE OF FELLOWSHIP AND THE LOCAL CHURCH 185

Chapter Seventeen JESUS WILL RETURN 209

Chapter Eighteen COMMUNION 221

Footnotes 252

Life Changing Principles for Victorious Living

Introduction

As you begin your new journey, I would like to share something with you. One time when I was going through a difficult season in my life, the Lord spoke to me. He said, "Shaun, don't just go through it, grow through it!"

That was a power word (thought) to my spirit. So I produce this work that as you study and absorb it, it will help you, 'Grow' through your life's journey with God, overcoming all and every obstacle in your way. Let's begin!

How do I begin to study God's Word?

(a)   Pray in the name of Jesus that God will give you His wisdom and understanding.

(b)   Read the Bible references for each study.

(c)   Try to memorise the scriptures that you have read.

(d) Finish your study by thanking God for the truths you have learned from His Word.

1. By receiving Jesus as Lord, you have become a son of God if you believe on His name - according to John 1:12. You now have the power residing in your spirit to become, be and do, all that God has planned for you and destined you to be.

2. If you have now become God's child, then He is now your Father. Read Romans 8:15-16.

    The Bible compares someone who has been born into the kingdom of God, as to a babe who has been born into this world, who needs milk to grow strong.

3. As a babe in Christ, you need to desire the sincere milk of the Word in order to grow, as in 1 Peter 2:2.

4. As your body needs the right food to grow strong physically, so you need to feed your inner man (spirit) the right food in order to grow strong spiritually. God's Word is spiritual food.

    John 6:63 says that the words that God speaks unto you are spirit and they are life.

    Jesus said, *"Man should not live by bread alone, but by each and every word that proceeds out of the mouth of God"* in Matthew 4:4.

    We find these Words by having a readiness of mind

and searching the scriptures as you will read in Acts 17:11.

In 2 Timothy 2:15, we are advised to, *"Study to show ourselves approved unto God, a workman that need not be ashamed, rightly dividing the word of truth."*

5. The Christian life is like driving a car! The Holy Spirit is our instructor, with us at the wheel learning to drive. We don't learn it all in one lesson, so as newborn babes, we can't always walk at our first attempt.

    We stumble, we fall, but our Father helps us up and says, 'Go again.' So the word of God (The Bible) is our road map to life.

6. If we do stumble or fall or get off the path or make a mistake or sin, we can pray to God to forgive us, and He will pick us up and put us back on track again.

    Read 1 John 1:9.

    Remember that God loves you, wants to bless and help you through life.

I pray that our Father, the God of our Lord Jesus Christ, the Father of Glory, may give unto you the spirit of revelation in the knowledge of Him. Ephesians 1:17.

Chapter One

BORN AGAIN - WHAT DOES IT MEAN?

John 3:1-8,

> "There was a man of the Pharisees, named Nicodemus, a ruler of the Jews. The same came to Jesus by night, and said unto Him, Rabbi, we know that Thou art a teacher come from God; for no man can do these miracles that Thou doest, except God be with Him.
>
> Jesus answered and said unto him, 'Truly, Truly, I say unto you, except a man be born again, he cannot see the kingdom of God'. Nicodemus saith unto Him, "How can a man be born when he is old? Can he enter the second time into his mother's womb, and be born?"
>
> Jesus answered, "Truly, Truly, I say unto you, except a man be born of water and of the Spirit, he cannot enter into the kingdom of God. That which is born of the flesh is flesh; and that which is born of the Spirit

is Spirit. Marvel not that I said unto you, you must be born again. The wind bloweth where it wills, and you hear the sound thereof, but cannot tell where it comes from, and where it goes: so is every one that is born of the Spirit."

From the above verses, we can see Jesus told one of the most religious men of His day, Nicodemus, that he must be born again in order for him to see the kingdom of God. Nicodemus had come to Jesus one night to enquire about this new teaching. Because he was a Pharisee and a ruler of the Jews, he believed in God. He prayed, fasted, tithed, and attended church services. He endeavoured to live righteously, yet even with all of these things going for him, Jesus still told him that in order to enter the kingdom of God, he must be born again.

You see, it is not by good works or good deeds or any act of righteousness that we have done, that saves us. We are saved according to His mercy by the washing of the new birth or regeneration and renewing of the Holy Spirit. (Titus 3:5, Author's Translation).

In the Book of Romans 3:23, it tells us every person has sinned (done bad things) and comes short of the glory of God. *"For the wages of sin is death, but the gift of God is eternal life through Jesus Christ our Lord"*, Romans 6:23. Here we can see that the wages of our sin is death, but the free gift of God is eternal life through Jesus Christ our Lord.

In Isaiah 64:6, it tells us that *"all our righteousness is as filthy rags"* in the sight of our God.

Romans 3:20-22 says,

> "Therefore, by the deeds of the law, there shall no flesh be justified in His sight: for by the law is the knowledge of sin. But now the righteousness of God without the law is manifested, being witnessed by the law and the prophets; even the righteousness of God which is by faith of Jesus Christ unto all and upon all them that believe: for there is no difference."

So let us just summarize the above to see what it means to be born again:

We have been born as babies and grown up to the age that we are now. During the course of our lives, all of us, without exception, have done something wrong. We have all made mistakes, because of our sin (mistakes) we were separated from God, spiritually dead and doomed to an eternity without God.

> "But God loved the world so much that He gave His only begotten Son, that whoever believes in Him should not perish but have everlasting life" (John 3:16).

Because of mankind's sin, God sent His Son, Jesus into the world, not to condemn the world, but that the world, that is to say, the people of the world, might be saved through Him. Jesus Christ came, and He lived a sinless life, and He went to the cross to pay the price for the transgressions (sins and wrongdoings, in the sight of God) of mankind.

In the Book of Isaiah 53:6 (Old Testament) it tells us that God laid on Jesus the iniquity of us all. In Isaiah 53:4-5, we can see that,

> *"Jesus bore our griefs, carried our sorrows, yet we did esteem Him stricken, smitten of God and afflicted, but He was wounded for our transgressions, He was bruised for our iniquities, the chastisement for our peace was upon Him, and by His stripes, we are healed."*

Every person had sinned. Sin results in death and eternal separation from God. That means without salvation, people will go to hell forever.

> *He answered and said unto them, "He that soweth the good seed is the Son of Man. The field is the world, the good seeds are the children of the kingdom, but the tares are the children of the wicked one. The enemy that sowed them is the devil, the harvest is the end of the world, and the reapers are the angels. As therefore the tares are gathered and burned in the fire, so shall it be in the end of this world."*

> *"The Son of man shall send forth His angels, and they shall gather out of His kingdom all things that offend, and them which do iniquity, and shall cast them into a furnace of fire. There shall be wailing and gnashing of teeth. Then shall the righteous shine forth as the sun in the kingdom of their Father. Who hath ears to hear, let him hear."* (Matthew 13:37-43).

Jesus Christ came to pay the price to bridge the gap, to buy us and bring us back to God, to give us eternal life, and to make us once again, God's children. You see, Jesus told Nicodemus, *"You must be born again."* We are born once, in our mother's womb (natural childbirth) born of water, but Jesus said we must be born again of the Holy Spirit in order to enter the kingdom of God. We have to make the decision - first realize that we have sinned and our sins have separated us from God and His blessings. Then we must choose to repent, to turn around from going our own way, to receive Jesus as our Lord and Saviour, and to follow God through obeying His Word and His will for our lives.

1 Peter 1:23 says: *"Being born again, not of corruptible seed, but of incorruptible, by the Word of God, which liveth and abideth forever."* The Word is the seed that comes into our heart and causes our faith to grow. Not only must we have God's Word in order to be born again, but we must have God's Spirit. It is not by works or righteousness that we have done, but according to His mercy, He has saved us by the washing and regeneration and renewing of the Holy Spirit (Titus 3:5). Jesus said in John 6:63, *" The Word that I speak unto you is spirit and it is life."*

How to Be Born Again

"For by grace are ye saved through faith, and that not of yourselves: it is the gift of God, Not of works, lest any man should boast." (Ephesians 2:8,9).

It is impossible to be saved except by the grace of God. We do not deserve it, based on our performance. It is God's power, working through His Word and Spirit that brings about new birth. Without an attitude of repentance and faith, God's power will not work in man's heart. Man must be obedient to God's will before he can receive God's blessings.

Believe and Confess - Romans 10:8-10 says,

> *"But what saith it? The Word is nigh thee, even in thy mouth, and in thy heart: that is, the Word of faith, which we preach; That if thou shalt confess with thy mouth the Lord Jesus, and shalt believe in thine heart that God hath raised Him from the dead, thou shalt be saved. For with the heart, man believeth unto righteousness: and with the mouth, confession is made unto salvation."* - our faith in God's Word expressed with our heart (**believe**) and with our mouth (**confess**).

Because we truly believe in our heart that God raised Jesus from the dead, there is no reason we should not be willing to confess Him as Lord. The moment someone believes in their heart upon Jesus and confesses Him as their Lord and Saviour, they are born again! They are saved!

> *"But as many as received Him, to them gave He the power to become the sons of God, even to them that believe on His name."* John 1:12.

A Brand New Creation

"Therefore if any man be in Christ, he is a new creature: old things are passed away, behold all things are become new" (2 Corinthians 5:17).

The new birth makes us a brand new creation. We are created after the image of Jesus Christ (Colossians 3:10). In our hearts (our spirit), we are made to be like Christ.

In order to live like Christ, we must *"...put on the new man, which is renewed in knowledge after the image of Him that created him"* (Colossians 3:10). This is done by **RENEWING THE MIND WITH GOD'S WORD**, and submitting our bodies to the authority of that Word (Romans 12:2, Ephesians 4:23-24).

My good friend Drummond Thom would always say, *"Before there can be a putting on, of the new man. We must first, put off the old."*

Translated Into God's Kingdom

*"Giving thanks unto the Father, which hath made us meet to be partakers of the inheritance of the saints in light: **WHO HATH DELIVERED US FROM THE POWER OF DARKNESS AND HATH TRANSLATED US INTO THE KINGDOM OF HIS DEAR SON**: in Whom we have redemption through His blood, even the forgiveness of sins."* (Colossians 1:12-14).

When we are born again, we are taken out of Satan's kingdom of darkness, and we are placed into the kingdom of Jesus, the kingdom of light. It is not something we just hope or wish for. It is a fact. The child of God does not have to be lorded over by Satan ever again. *"If the Son, therefore, shall make you free, ye shall be free indeed"* (John 8:36).

The Law of the Spirit of Life

This new kingdom is a spiritual kingdom, but just because salvation is basically a spiritual rebirth does not mean that it has no effect on our bodies, minds, or everyday living. It can and should have a great impact on every part of our lives.

In every age and culture, there are certain rules and laws that govern the actions of the inhabitants of that area. It is the same in spiritual life. There are laws for those in Satan's kingdom, and there are laws for those in God's kingdom. The new birth gives us a new law. **"FOR THE LAW OF THE SPIRIT OF LIFE IN CHRIST JESUS** *hath made me free from the law of sin and death"* (Romans 8:2).

The law of life includes love, joy, peace, happiness, prosperity, abundance, health, contentment, and blessings. These provisions are made for the Christian in the New Covenant. We must enforce them in our lives. As we enforce them, God will back us. He always enforces His Word, which is true and never changes. His Word is law and forever settled in heaven.

Forgiveness of All Our Sins

The day we make Jesus our Lord and Saviour we are forgiven

of all our sins, in fact, we were legally forgiven when Jesus gave His life as a ransom for us. But we do not experience that forgiveness until we receive it by faith.

Although a person may have committed many sins, the chief sin of the unsaved is **NOT BELIEVING ON CHRIST** (John 16:9). When a person gets that straightened out, the root of the problem is solved. The blood of Christ cleanses the heart the moment a person believes and confesses Him as Saviour. Thus all past sins are remitted or taken away by the powerful cleansing work of His blood (1 John 1:7). *"... We have redemption through His blood, the forgiveness of sins, according to the riches of His grace."* (Ephesians 1:7).

Here is a simple prayer you can pray in order to be born again:

Father, I come before you in the precious name of Jesus.
Lord, I have made mistakes in my life.
Father, I acknowledge that I have sinned.
I see in Your Word it says that Jesus died for my sins. Please forgive me of all of my sins and mistakes against you that I have committed, or any other person that I may have wronged.
I forgive all those who have sinned against me or wronged me in any way.
Father, I repent right now of my sins.
Father, I thank You that You sent Jesus, who came in the flesh and died for me, taking my sins on the cross, shedding His blood for me. Thank

you, I am now clean from my sins, through the shed blood of Jesus Christ. Thank you that on the third day You rose Jesus again from the dead. Jesus now sits at Your right hand in all power and glory, as King and Lord of all.

Jesus, please come into my life, my heart, right now by the Person and power of the Holy Spirit, and make me born again.
Jesus, I receive You now as my Lord and my Saviour. Amen.

Welcome to God's Family

If you prayed this simple prayer, you can know, according to God's Word that you are saved. You are now born again and have become a Christian, a follower of Christ. You must stand on His Word, not your feelings, emotions, or anything else. It is God's Word that guarantees your salvation.

Assurance of Salvation

"And this is the record that God has given to us eternal life, and this life is in His Son. **HE THAT HAS THE SON HAS LIFE**, *and he that has not the Son of God has not life. These things have I written unto you that believe on the name of the Son of God;* **THAT YOU MAY KNOW** *that ye have eternal life, and that ye may* **BELIEVE ON THE NAME** *of the Son of God."* (1 John 5: 11-13).

The Resurrection and the Life

Jesus said, "I am the Resurrection and the Life. He that believeth in Me, though he were dead, yet shall he live. And whosoever liveth and believeth in Me shall never die." (John 11:25-26).

Isn't that wonderful? I encourage all who read this to embrace this truth from the Word of God. Today, receive Jesus Christ as your personal Lord and Saviour. Your name will then be found in the Lord's Book of Life. (Revelation 3:5, 20:15 & Luke 10:20).

BORN AGAIN - WHAT DOES IT MEAN? REVISION

I have found that one of the most powerful ways to learn God's Word is to memorize verses. The Bible says to keep God's Word before your eyes and in the middle of your heart. We could say in the middle of your focus of attention.

1. Write out and memorize Romans 3:23.

   ....

   ....

   ....

2. Write out and memorize Romans 6:23.

   ....

   ....

   ....

3. Write out and memorize I John 1:9.

    ....

    ....

    ....

4. In a few short words, answer the following question: How do you know you are saved?

    ....

    ....

    ....

    ....

   N.B. There are now many translations of the Holy Bible (God's Word). I still prefer the Authorized King James Version and use it most of the time. I find it very easy to memorize scripture from. But you can purchase a version that you are comfortable with, to study and memorize scripture.

Chapter Two

LORDSHIP OF JESUS

☙ ❧

What does the Lordship of Jesus actually mean?

How does it relate to you and me?

We will find the answers to these questions as we examine the Word of God closely. Remember that to become a child of God, you had to receive Jesus as your Lord. The Oxford Dictionary defines the word 'Lord' as master, ruler, and owner. So actually, what has happened is that you have given Jesus to be the owner, ruler, and master of your life. He has become your Lord, we might say 'Boss' and as 'Boss', what He says, goes. Where people, who have endeavoured to live the Christian life have failed, is that they have taken back the position of Lord (for themselves) and only allowed Jesus to be their Saviour.

IF YOU ALLOW JESUS TO BE YOUR LORD, YOU WILL NEVER FAIL.

Read Luke 6:46-49 carefully:
"But why do you call Me Lord, Lord, and do not do

the things which I say? Whoever comes to Me, and hears my sayings and does them, I will show you who he is like: He is like a man building a house who dug deep and laid the foundation on the rock. And when the flood arose, the stream beat vehemently against that house, and could not shake it, for it was founded on the rock. But he who heard and did nothing is like a man who built a house on the earth without a foundation, against which the stream beat vehemently; and immediately it fell. And the ruin of that house was great."

1. It is one thing to say that Jesus is your Lord, but for Jesus to be your Lord, you must do the things that he says (verse 46). In these few verses of scripture, Jesus compares the Christian life to someone who builds a house. A house has to be designed, blueprinted, and built. God is the designer, the Bible is the blueprint, but we have to build it. Of the two men that built, one was successful, the other failed.

2. (a) One succeeded because he came to the Lord, heard what he said and did it. (verse 47).

    (b) The other failed because he heard the Lord but did not do what he said, and is likened to one without a foundation, thereby causing the ruin of that house. (verse 49).

3. If we want to build successfully, and have our house stand and not come to ruin when the floods (tests, trials, and temptations of Satan) come our way, we must be *"doers of the*

word, and not hearers only, thereby deceiving ourselves", as in James 1:22.

The man in Luke 6:48 who *"dug deep"* is the same as he, who in James 1:25, *"looked into the perfect law of liberty"*. He searched and studied the Word of God.

4. Read James 1:25 carefully:

"But he who looks into the perfect law of liberty and continues in it, and is not a forgetful hearer but a doer of the work, this one will be blessed in what he does."

    (a)   We are not to be a 'forgetful hearer'.
    (b)   We are to be a doer of the word.
    (c)   The result of hearing and doing is that we will be blessed in our deed.

Jesus Wants to Live His Life Through Us

He wants to be president not just resident. We use the example of the Christian life to that of driving a car. Picture the car as your life, and you at the wheel, steering your life wherever you will. Before you accepted Jesus as your Lord, you were alone, going and doing whatever you wished. But the moment that you received Jesus, He came into your life (car) to direct and help you live the life that God has planned for you. He wants to live His life through you, but for Him to do this, you have to be doing things His way.

5. Read Galatians 2:20 carefully:
"I have been crucified with Christ; it is no longer I

who live, but Christ lives in me; and the life which I now live in the flesh I live by faith in the Son of God, who loved me and gave himself for me."

    (a)   "I" no longer live.
    (b)   Christ now lives in me instead.
    (c)   The life I now live, I live by faith of the Son of God.
    (d)   Faith comes by hearing. Romans 10:17 says, *"Faith comes by hearing, and hearing by the word of God."*

SO WE MIGHT SAY *"THE LIFE I NOW LIVE, I LIVE BY HEARING THE WORD OF GOD AND DOING IT."*

As we do what He instructs, He becomes our ruler. He has that right, being our owner, our Lord.

6.   To 'buy' us, back from the kingdom of darkness, Jesus paid an awesome price:

    (a)   Acts 20:28 says, *"Take heed therefore unto yourselves, and to all the flock over the which the Holy Spirit hath made you overseers, to feed the church of God, which He hath purchased with His own blood."*

    (b)   John 10:11 says, *"I am the good shepherd: the good shepherd giveth his life for the sheep."*

7.   As we are obedient in serving Him, He becomes our master, and as master, He is able to meet all of our needs. (Luke 17:12-15).

LORDSHIP OF JESUS
REVISION

1. In your own words, give a brief understanding of what it means to have Jesus Lord of your life.

   ....

   ....

   ....

2. Write out and memorize Galatians 2:20.

   ....

   ....

3. Mankind was redeemed, bought back to God by the?

   ....

   ....

   ....

CHAPTER THREE

WATER BAPTISM

One of the last statements that Jesus made, just before ascending to heaven was, *"Go make disciples of all nations, baptizing them in the name of the Father and of the Son and of the Holy Spirit."* For Jesus to institute Water Baptism, it must be very important in our walk with God.

WATER BAPTISM SHOULD NOT BE TAKEN LIGHTLY. IT WAS INSTITUTED AND COMMANDED BY OUR LORD JESUS CHRIST.

What does Water Baptism mean? The word 'Baptism' comes from the Greek word BAPTIZO, which means:

(1) To dip (as to dye a garment), immerse.
(2) To cause to perish (drowning a man, sinking a ship).

Water Baptism does not save you. You are saved when you make the decision to receive Jesus as your Lord and Saviour, and are then born again.

You may ask yourself "Why should I be baptised? I am born again, I'm on my way to heaven. What is the need for baptism?" If, for no other reason Christians or disciples should be baptised, because as we can see in Matthew 28:19, our Lord commanded us to baptise His followers. Another reason as to why a believer should be baptised is to identify with Christ as God's Son.

In Matthew 3:17, we read that as Jesus was baptised the Father spoke saying, *"This is My beloved Son"*. As we go through the waters of baptism, our Father's voice echoes in our heart the reassurance that I am His child, born of His Spirit, I am His Son, just as Jesus is.

Remember that water Baptism does not save you. You were saved when you received Jesus as your Lord.

What is Water Baptism?

IT IS AN OUTWARD SIGN OF AN INWARD GRACE.

Believers' Water Baptism corresponds to Jewish circumcision. The reason for circumcision to the Jews as it says in Genesis 17:11 is that it was a token (outward sign) of the covenant between God and His people.

> *"And ye shall circumcise the flesh of your foreskin; and it shall be a token of the covenant betwixt me and you."* Genesis 17:11.

In the Old Testament, Abraham received the sign of circumcision, as it says in Romans 4:11,

> "And he received the sign of circumcision, a seal of the righteousness of the faith which he had yet being uncircumcised; that he might be the father of all them that believe, though they be not circumcised; that righteousness might be imputed unto them also."

In Genesis 17:12 in the Old Testament, circumcision took place on the 8th day. Circumcision on the 8th day was a sign of the covenant with God. Number eight (8) in Bible numerics means **'NEW LIFE'**. So then, now to the Christian, those who are born again, water baptism takes the place of the Jewish circumcision. Water baptism is an outward sign of the covenant between you and your God that's in your heart.

Baptism is the Sign of Our New Life in Christ

> Romans 3:22 says, *"Even the righteousness of God, which is by faith of Jesus Christ unto all and upon all them that believe; for there is no difference;"*.

As we are water baptised, we also identify with Christ in His death, burial and resurrection. It is a pictorial of our being crucified with Christ, buried with Him and rising to new life. When we are born again, we are new creations 'in Christ Jesus'.

Therefore, because we are in Christ Jesus, God sees us -

(a)   At Jesus' crucifixion, as crucified with Christ, as in

Galatians 2:20, *"I am crucified with Christ: nevertheless, I live; yet not I, but Christ liveth in me: and the life which I now live in the flesh I live by the faith of the Son of God, who loved me, and gave himself for me."*

(b)   At His burial, as buried with Christ into death, as in Romans 6:4, *"Therefore, we are buried with him by baptism into death: that like as Christ was raised up from the dead by the glory of the Father, even so we also should walk in newness of life."*

(c)   At His Resurrection, as risen with Christ, as in Colossians 2:12, *"Buried with Him in baptism, wherein also ye are risen with him through the faith of the operation of God, who hath raised him from the dead."*

Therefore, baptism is to identify with Christ in His death, burial and resurrection.

BAPTISM OF A BELIEVER IN WATER IS A PHYSICAL EXAMPLE OF THE SPIRITUAL EVENT OF THE SPIRIT OF MAN BEING BAPTISED INTO THE BODY OF CHRIST (THAT IS: BEING BORN AGAIN).

A believer should be water baptised, according to Acts 16:33, 'straightway'. Referring to the jailer (a new believer) and Paul and Silas, it says, *"And he took them the same hour of the night, and washed their stripes; and was baptised, he and all his, straightway."*

In the Word of God it says a believer should be baptised *"in the name of the Father, and of the Son, and of the Holy Spirit,"* (Matthew 28:19) *"in the name of Jesus Christ"* (Acts 2:38).

N.B. Colossians 2:9 says: *"In Christ dwells all the fullness of the Godhead bodily."* Philippians 2:9 says that God has given Him a name that is above every name. Therefore, seeing the Godhead (Father, Son, and Holy Spirit) abides in Christ, then His name incorporates the name of the Godhead.

Certain conditions are to be met before water baptism.

> In Romans 10:9 it reads, *"That if thou shalt confess with thy mouth the Lord Jesus, and shalt believe in thine heart that God hath raised Him from the dead, thou shalt be saved."*
>
> Acts 8:37 tells us, *"If thou believest with all thine heart thou mayest."* And he answered and said, *"I believe that Jesus Christ is the Son of God."*

Therefore, believing in the heart and confessing with the mouth (in fact the born again experience) are conditions necessary before water baptism.

WATER BAPTISM REVISION

1. Write out and memorize Matthew 28:19.

   ....
   ....
   ....

2. What was the point of Jewish circumcision in the Old Testament (Genesis 17:11)?

   ....
   ....
   ....

3. In your own words, describe why water baptism is important to a believer?

   ....
   ....
   ....

Chapter Four

BAPTISM OF THE SPIRIT

༄ ༅

The baptism of the Spirit can also be referred to as being filled with the Spirit. When we are born again, we are born of the Spirit of God. In John 20:22, we see Jesus after His resurrection, breathing on His disciples, and He said unto them, *"Receive ye the Holy Spirit."* Here, the disciples were born again, but in Acts 1:4-8, Jesus instructed His disciples to wait in Jerusalem until they be baptised, or as we can say, filled with the Holy Spirit.

> *"And being assembled together with them, commanded them that they should not depart from Jerusalem, but wait for the promise of the Father, which, saith He, ye have heard of Me. For John truly baptised with water; but ye shall be baptised with the Holy Spirit not many days hence. When they therefore were come together, they asked of Him saying, 'Lord, wilt Thou at this time restore again the kingdom to Israel?' And He said unto them, 'It is not for you to*

know the times or the seasons, which the Father hath put in His own power. <u>But you shall receive power, after that the Holy Spirit is come upon you:</u> and you shall be witnesses unto me both in Jerusalem and in all Judea, and in Samaria, and unto the uttermost part of the earth.'"

Divine Empowerment

The disciples had already received the Holy Spirit, or were born again of the Holy Spirit, but now Jesus told them they could be filled with the Holy Spirit. He went on to say that this infilling would give them the power to witness to His resurrection.

In Ephesians 5:18, Paul instructs us to be filled with the Holy Spirit, *"And be not drunk with wine, wherein is excess; but be filled with the Spirit."*

As we study God's Word, we can see that the baptism in the Spirit did many things to the disciples. Three of them stand out above the others. This experience:-

1. gave them power to win souls;
2. gave them power to heal the sick;
3. gave them power to withstand persecution.

In all these things, they walked in the comfort and power of the Holy Spirit. No one knows the importance of the Holy Spirit like God does. God commanded the disciples to 'tarry until' they were endued with power from on High. We are exhorted in 1 Corinthians 12 and 14 to covet earnestly, to earnestly desire spiritual gifts. Paul says I want all of you to speak in tongues. We must covet this gift earnestly, use it regularly, building ourselves up. Tongues is the doorway to the nine gifts of the Spirit, the treasures God has for His church.

We receive this precious gift, the ability to speak in unknown tongues, when we are filled with the Holy Spirit.

> John the Baptist in Luke 3:16: *"I indeed baptise you with water; but one mightier than I cometh, the latchet of whose shoes I am not worthy to unloose; He shall baptise you with the Holy Spirit and with fire."*

Jesus is Alive

So we could say, the main purpose of the baptism of the Spirit is to proclaim with evidence that Jesus is alive.

The main condition in order to be filled with the Spirit one must be born again. In John 14:17 it tells us: *"Even the Spirit of truth; whom the world cannot receive, because it seeth Him not, neither knoweth Him; but ye know Him; for He dwelleth with you, and shall be in you."* The world, that is to say, the unsaved, cannot receive the infilling of the Holy Spirit, only believers who have first been born again can be filled with the Spirit.

> In John 7:37-39, *"In the last day, that great day of the feast, Jesus stood and cried, saying 'If any man thirst, let him come unto Me, and drink. He that believeth on Me, as the scripture hath said - out of his belly shall flow rivers of living water.' (But this spake He of the Spirit, which they that believe on Him should receive; for the Holy Spirit was not yet given, because that Jesus was not yet glorified)."*

Jesus said that he that believed on Him, out of his belly (refers to spirit/inner man) would flow rivers of living water. Here Jesus said He was referring to the Holy Spirit, which they would believe on Him to receive.

> In Acts 2:38, Peter told the people, *"Repent and be baptised every one of you in the name of Jesus Christ for the remission of sins* (water baptism), *and ye shall receive the gift of the Holy Spirit* (that is, to be filled with the Spirit).*"*

> In Acts 2:4, we read that, *"they were all filled with the Holy Spirit, and began to speak with other tongues, as the Spirit gave them utterance."* These are the tongues that they spoke. It was a language that was foreign to them and unknown to their natural mind. We will discuss *"tongues"* in more detail later in this lesson.

> In the Book of Acts 10:44-48, we see another example of people being filled with the Holy Spirit, and speaking in other tongues:

> "While Peter yet spake these words, the Holy Spirit fell on all them which heard the Word. And they of the circumcision which believed were astonished, as many as came with Peter, because that on the Gentiles also was poured out the gift of the Holy Spirit. For they heard them speak with tongues, and magnify God. Then answered Peter, 'Can any man forbid water, that these should not be baptised, which have received the Holy Spirit as well as we?" And he commanded them to be baptised in the name of the Lord. Then prayed they him to tarry certain days."

In the Book of Mark 16:17, it says,

> "And these signs shall follow them that believe; In My name shall they cast out devils; they shall speak with new tongues." Jesus said, one of the signs that would follow the believer is that they would speak with new tongues."

How to be Filled With the Spirit

James 1:17, "Every good gift and every perfect gift is from above, and cometh down from the Father of lights, with whom is no variableness, neither shadow of turning." Here, the Word of God tells us that every good gift and every perfect gift comes down from our Father. God has many wonderful blessings for His children.

> Acts 2:39, *"For the promise is unto you, and to your children, and to all that are afar off, even as many as the Lord our God shall call."*

Remember, it is a command of God *"to be filled with the Spirit."* Ephesians 5:18.

> Luke 11:11-13, *"If a son shall ask bread of any of you that is a father, will he give him a stone? Or if he ask a fish, will he for a fish give him a serpent? Or if he shall ask an egg, will he offer him a scorpion? If ye then, being evil, know how to give good gifts unto your children; how much more shall your heavenly Father give the Holy Spirit to them that ask Him?"* If you are born again, here we can see, it is the Father's desire to give the Holy Spirit to those that ask Him.

Pray this simple prayer.

> **"My heavenly Father, I am a believer. I am Your child and You are my Father. Jesus is my Lord. I believe with all my heart that Your Word is true. Your Word says that if I will ask I will receive the Holy Spirit, so in the name of Jesus Christ, my Lord, I am asking You to fill me to overflowing with Your precious Holy Spirit.**
>
> **Jesus, please baptise me in the Holy Spirit. Because of Your Word, I believe that I now receive and I thank You for it.**

I believe that the Holy Spirit is within me, and by faith, I accept it.

Now Holy Spirit, rise up within me as I praise my God. I fully expect to speak with other tongues as You give me the utterance." In Jesus name!

Now, I want you to begin to thank God and praise Him for filling you with the Holy Spirit. As you do, there will rise up within your spirit certain words and syllables that are unknown to you, so by faith speak. Don't speak any more English (or your native tongue). You can't speak two languages at the same time. Just begin to speak the syllables that are on your lips. You are like a baby, and you will begin by speaking baby-sounding words. (Remember, you have to use your own voice. God will not force you to speak.)

From this moment on, you are a Spirit-filled believer. Jesus said in John 14:16, *"I will pray the Father, and He shall give you another Comforter, that He may abide with you forever."* The Holy Spirit is your Comforter, which means Counsellor, Helper, Intercessor, Advocate, Strengthener, Standby. You can rely on Him to fulfil all these areas of ministry.

The Holy Spirit was sent to teach you all things, to lead and guide you into all truth (John 14:26, 16:12,13). You are no longer alone. The Holy Spirit is the Comforter who will abide with you forever!

BAPTISM OF THE SPIRIT REVISION

1. What is the first condition that must be met in order for a person to receive the Holy Spirit?

   ....

   ....

   ....

2. Is the baptism of the Spirit a separate experience to being born again?   *Yes or No*

3. Is the Baptism of the Spirit the same as the Baptism of water?   *Yes or No*

4. Write out and memorize Ephesians 5:18.

   ....

   ....

   ....

5. According to Mark 16:17, list some of the signs that should follow believers.

   ....

   ....

   ....

Chapter Five

TONGUES

After you have asked the Father in the name of Jesus to fill you with His Spirit, according to the Word of God, you are now filled with the Spirit. You now have the ability, God's power within you, to enable you to speak a language out of your spirit you have never learned. Just as English (or your native tongue) is the voice of your mind, so praying in the Spirit is the voice of your spirit. It is your spirit that is in direct communication with God.

> 1 Corinthians 14:2 says: *"For he that speaketh in an unknown tongue speaketh not unto men, but unto God; for no man understandeth him; howbeit in the spirit he speaketh mysteries."*

Your natural mind will not understand the words that you are speaking, for it is not coming from your natural mind, but from your spirit.

1 Corinthians 14:14 says: *"For if I pray in an unknown tongue, my spirit prayeth, but my understanding is unfruitful."*

Pray with the Spirit

So then you can now pray in your native language, the language you learned when you were a baby, and you can also pray in your new heavenly language.

1 Corinthians 14:15 says: *"What is it then? I will pray with the spirit, and I will pray with the understanding also: I will sing with the spirit, and I will sing with the understanding also."*

When you first get filled with the Spirit and begin to speak with other tongues, your natural mind can argue with you that you are making these words up. This is where faith comes in. You have to trust that once you have asked the Father for this gift, He has given you the gift. You then take the step of faith and begin to speak out sounds and or syllables (words) that come up from your spirit and out through your mouth.

In my experience, while assisting people in releasing this new heavenly prayer language of tongues, I have found people receive the gift to different degrees. But as they speak and exercise the gift, the words increase and the flow becomes bolder and fluent.

Sharing my own experience and that of my wife's, we both received in different ways and to different degrees. I received many words and what I describe as a full flow, a new heavenly language. My wife, on the other hand, only received a couple of syllables, but as she spoke them over and over and out loud, more words came.

I liken it to a baby when it first starts to speak. It starts with a few syllables until he or she forms them into words. As the baby chatters more, the sounds and words become clearer and a language is formed and released.

Over time my wife developed a full heavenly language and now speaks fluently in tongues, and has done so for many years now.

So I want to encourage you, when you first receive the gift, whether like me, you get a full language or like my wife, you start with a couple of words, keep speaking. As you speak in tongues, exercising your faith, that you are speaking as the Holy Spirit leads, you will build yourself up and enjoy a supernatural release of faith and refreshing, that only the Holy Spirit can bring.

Encouragement

It is good to get with other Spirit-filled Christians that can assist you to speak in tongues, releasing this precious gift. With a couple of other Christians, speaking in tongues with you, you will find it easier at first, to release this gift by joining in and speaking in tongues with them. Everyone together can speak in tongues to God and all are edified. I also encourage people that after they have received the baptism of the Spirit and speak in tongues, to do so when they are driving their car, going for a walk or having a shower etc. In this way, people can overcome any feelings of embarrassment, by developing and exercising this gift when in a safe and appropriate environment.

The Purpose of Tongues

God by His Holy Spirit has given you this new language to edify your spirit man, or we could say, charge up, build up and strengthen your spirit man.

> 1 Corinthians 14:4 - *"He that speaketh in an unknown tongue edifieth himself; but he that prophesieth edifieth the church."*

> Jude 20 - *"But ye, beloved, building up yourselves on your most holy faith, praying in the Holy Spirit."*

Remember, when you are praying in the spirit, you are speaking directly to the Almighty God. At times, we do not always know what to pray, in some circumstances, with the natural mind. We might not know or understand all of the situations that are affecting us or our friends or whatever else we are going to pray for. In which case, with our natural mind, we would not know exactly how to pray God's will for the situation, but we are guaranteed in Romans 8:26 & 27 that if we pray in the spirit, that is to say, pray in tongues, we can pray the perfect will of God for any given situation.

> *"Likewise, the Spirit also helpeth our infirmities; for we know not what we should pray for as we ought;*

> *but the Spirit himself maketh intercession for us with groanings which cannot be uttered. And He that searcheth the hearts knoweth what is the mind of the Spirit, because He maketh intercession for the saints according to the will of God."* (Romans 8:26-27).

For it is the Holy Spirit who will make intercession through us in other tongues according to the perfect will of God.

What a powerful thought! What a powerful revelation! Praying in and with the Spirit is a prayer of pure faith based on the perfect will of God, because the prayer didn't originate with you. It originated with God! It originated in the realm of the spirit and comes forth birthed by the Holy Spirit through your tongue, the perfect answer or outcome, the will of God for that situation or circumstance. Can there be a better, more rewarding way to pray?

Also in Isaiah 28:11-12 in the Old Testament,

> *"For with stammering lips and another tongue will he speak to this people. To whom he said, This is the rest wherewith ye may cause the weary to rest; and this is the refreshing: yet they would not hear."*

It tells us that praying in the spirit (other tongues) is a rest and a refreshing, strengthening or renewing for the spirit. Remember, Jesus tells us in Mark 16:17 that one of the signs that follow the believer is that they will speak with new tongues.

Praying in the spirit also enlarges our comprehension or understanding of the Word of God (Ephesians 3:16 19). By praying in the spirit, we release the faith contained in the Word of God as we release God's wisdom and revelation knowledge in us. (1 Corinthians 2: 12-13).

Praying God's Perfect Will

Satan hates it when we pray in the spirit, for as we pray God's perfect will by praying as the Holy Spirit directs, we damage the kingdom of darkness.

> *And these signs shall follow them that believe; In my name shall they cast out devils; they shall speak with new tongues;* (Mark 16:17).

We are living in the days of the outpouring of God's Spirit on all flesh. God promises to pour out His Spirit upon all flesh. He promises visions and dreams and supernatural gifts of the Spirit. He says, His followers, the new believer, will speak with tongues.

Praying in tongues is one of the most precious and powerful gifts of the Holy Spirit to empower your walk with God. I believe it is the key to flowing in the other gifts. If you don't have this gift, ask for it, strongly desire it and God will give it to you. Now rejoice and receive in the name of Jesus. Acts 2:16-18.

TONGUES REVISION

1. According to the last lesson, we learnt that the Holy Spirit is our comforter, which means in the Greek:

    a..

    b..

    c..

    d..

    e..

    f..

2. One of the ways in which the Holy Spirit strengthens us, is when we?

    ....

    ....

    ....

3. The Father God by His Holy Spirit has given you the ability to pray in tongues so you can?

    a..
    b..
    c..your spirit man.

4. Sometimes we are not sure how or what to pray for a person or situation, but we can pray in tongues and know we are praying God's...

....

5. Write out and memorize Romans 8:26 & 27.

....

....

....

6. According to Isaiah 28:11-12, praying the Spirit gives the believer-

   a) ....

   b) ....

CHAPTER SIX

YOU ARE THE RIGHTEOUSNESS OF GOD IN CHRIST

Righteousness, simply defined, is RIGHT STANDING WITH GOD. It gives a person the ability to be free of guilt, condemnation, fear, and inferiority. These four problems rob many Christians of God's blessings. It is easy to see why an understanding of righteousness could transform a person's life. Imagine no guilt, no condemnation, and no inferiority. What a blessed life that would be!

Righteousness is a Gift

There is a world of difference in a man's self-righteousness and the gift of righteousness from God. Self-righteousness boasts in itself, but the gift of righteousness can boast only in the finished work of Christ.

> *"For if by one man's offence death reigned by one, much more they which receive abundance of grace and of the **GIFT OF RIGHTEOUSNESS** shall reign in life by one, Jesus Christ"* (Romans 5:17).

Jesus Bore our Sin - Unrighteousness

The human race owed a tremendous debt of sin. Because mankind was unable to pay its debt, God sent His own Son to pay for it (1 Peter 2:24). Jesus was our substitute. He took our place. He paid the awful price for our sin. He did it because He loved us (John 3:16-17).

Now that the debt is paid, when we believe, we receive right standing with God. It is actually the right standing that Jesus earned as a result of His obedience unto death. We receive His righteousness the moment we take Him as our Lord and Saviour.

"For He hath made Him to be sin for us, who knew no sin; that we might be made the righteousness of God in Him" (2 Corinthians 5:21).

If Christ dwells in our hearts by faith, God's power goes into operation and makes us the righteousness of God, in Him.

Righteousness for Everyone Who Believes

We struggle with the idea of being righteous because we are all well acquainted with the Scriptures declaring man's sinfulness. The gift of righteousness is available to all who believe in Jesus Christ. Satan and the powers of darkness, regularly like to remind us of all the sins we have committed. We must now renew to the truths revealed in God's Word, concerning our righteousness.

> "But now the righteousness of God without the law is manifested, being witnessed by the Law and the Prophets. Even **THE RIGHTEOUSNESS OF GOD, WHICH IS BY FAITH** of Jesus Christ, unto all and upon all them that believe. For there is no difference: For all have sinned, and come short of the glory of God; Being justified freely by His grace through the redemption that is in Christ Jesus." (Romans 3:21-24).

Receiving Righteousness by Faith

Righteousness is actually received at salvation. Because many have not understood the righteousness of God, which is by faith, they have failed to experience the full joy of this great gift.

The message of righteousness is good news. The moment we hear this word, it should cause faith to rise in our heart. We want to receive it. It is ours - a gift from God. We must BELIEVE and CONFESS IT, to POSSESS IT.

> "For with the heart man believeth unto **RIGHTEOUSNESS**; and with the mouth, confession is made unto salvation" (Romans 10:10).

No Condemnation or Guilt

A sense of righteousness gives us confidence that God has truly forgiven us of our sins. We begin to see that the judgment and condemnation that we deserved, fell on Jesus. We have been justified (declared not guilty) because of the blood of Christ that was shed for us (Romans 5:9).

> *"There is therefore now **NO CONDEMNATION** to them which are in Christ Jesus, who walk not after the flesh, but after the Spirit."* (Romans 8:1).

We are freed from sin, with all its guilt and condemnation, so that we may become the **SERVANTS OF RIGHTEOUSNESS** (Romans 6:18).

By an act of faith, we begin to think not of our sins and shortcomings, but of our righteousness in Christ. Why should we continue to think and talk about our unworthiness? When we have been made worthy by Jesus Christ. He has qualified us to *"be partakers of the inheritance of the saints in light"* (Colossians 1:12). It is not our works but our faith in His works.

No Fear

Righteousness is right standing with God. If I am in right standing with God, then He is not fighting against me. He is on my side. He is for me. He desires my best.

What joy will fill our hearts the day we realize *"If God be for us, who can be against us?"* (Romans 8:31). We have nothing to fear. David said, *"The Lord is my light and my salvation; whom shall I fear? The Lord is the strength of my life; of whom shall I be afraid?"* (Psalms 27:1).

God has given us the gift of righteousness because of His love for us.

"There is no fear in love; but perfect love casteth out fear: because fear hath torment. He that feareth is not made perfect in love" (1 John 4:18).

A loving father does not want his children to be so fearful of him that they are afraid to talk to him. He desires their respect, reverence, and obedience, but he wants them to feel comfortable coming to him. God invites us to *"come boldly unto the throne of grace that we may obtain mercy and find grace to help in time of need"* (Hebrews 4:16). *"For God hath not given us the spirit of fear; but of power, and of love, and of a sound mind"* (2 Timothy 1:7). No Inferiority.

Reign in Life

Occasionally when someone is asked how they are doing, we hear them respond with these words: "Under the circumstances, I think I'll make it." As Christians, thank God, we do not have to be 'under the circumstances', in fact, after we receive the abundance of God's grace and His gift of righteousness, we are to reign in this life by Jesus Christ.

Because I have a right standing with God, I do not have to feel inferior to the powers of Satan. I am an heir of God and a joint-heir with Christ (Romans 8:17). As we receive the righteousness of God, we become partakers of the divine nature of God (2 Peter 1:4). His strength has become our strength. His ability is our ability. His life is our life.

> *"I am crucified with Christ: Nevertheless I live; yet not I, but CHRIST LIVETH IN ME: and the life which I now live in the flesh I LIVE BY THE FAITH OF THE SON OF GOD, who loved me and gave himself for me"* (Galatians 2:20).

Continual Cleansing from Unrighteousness

As Christians, we may miss the mark and sin. Sin is unrighteousness. It is not pleasing to God. It must be dealt with. The best time to do this is immediately, if not sooner. Do not wait to repent, just repent!

> The promise of God is, *"If we confess our sins, He is faithful and just to* **FORGIVE US OUR SINS**, *and to* **CLEANSE US FROM ALL UNRIGHTEOUSNESS"** *(1 John 1:9).* *"...the* **BLOOD** *of Jesus Christ His Son* **CLEANSETH** *us from all sin"* (1 John 1:7).

Our Prayers are Effective

With a right standing with God, we can come boldly into His presence with our praises and petitions (Hebrews 4:16). One of the most important things we must do as we enter into God's presence is to be sure our hearts are cleansed from all sin. This comes by faith in the cleansing power of the blood of Christ. After we know we are cleansed, we can have confidence in our prayers.

> *"Beloved, if our heart condemn us not, then have we confidence towards God"* (1 John 3:21).

God delights in hearing the prayers of His righteous children. *"For the eyes of the Lord are over the righteous, and His ears are open unto their prayers: but the face of the Lord is against them that do evil"* (1 Peter 3:12). Evidently, if we are not righteous or if we are not seeking God's righteousness, our prayers will not be very effective.

Thank God, *"The effectual fervent prayer of a righteous man availeth much"* (James 5:16). God will hear and answer our prayers if we maintain our right standing (righteousness in Christ) by faith.

YOU ARE THE RIGHTEOUSNESS OF GOD IN CHRIST REVISION

1. Write out and memorize Romans 5:17.

   ....

   ....

   ....

2. Righteousness can simply be defined as:

   ....

   ....

3. Jesus paid the price in full for our sins, leaving nothing left for us to pay.   *True or False.*

4. We can earn righteousness by good works. *True or False.*

5. We cannot earn righteousness. It is a free gift of God. *True or False.*

6. When you received Christ as your Lord and Saviour, you were made the righteousness of God in Him. *True or False.*

7. You have just as much right as Jesus Christ because of what he has done for you, to come boldly to the throne of God.   *True or False.*

Chapter Seven

PRAYER

Prayer is simply talking with God, not only in church, or when you are facing a difficult situation, but prayer is for any time, anywhere. In 1 Thessalonians 5:17, we are instructed to pray without ceasing.

> I Timothy 2:1-4, *Here we are exhorted first of all that we "make supplications, prayers, intercessions and giving of thanks for all men, for kings and for all that are in authority, that we may lead quiet and peaceable lives in all godliness and honesty". It goes on to say, "this is good and acceptable in the sight of God, our Saviour, for it is His will that all men be saved and come to the knowledge of the truth."*

Not only then can we, or should we pray for our own needs to be met, but we should also pray for the needs of others. In Galatians 6:2, we are instructed to *"bear one another's burden, and so fulfil the law of Christ."* So then we can bring our own needs to our Father through Jesus, and we can also pray for the needs of others in His name. Prayer then is a privilege, but not only is prayer a privilege, but prayer is a powerful and mighty force.

In Mark 11:24, Jesus tells us *"that whatsoever things we desire when we pray, if we believe that we receive, we shall have them."* Here we can see, it is God's will and desire to answer the good and right prayers of our heart.

In James 5:16, we read, *"The effectual fervent* (heartfelt continued) *prayer of a righteous man availeth much* (makes tremendous power available)." It is dynamic in its working. Through prayer, we fellowship with our Father. Any relationship is established and grows through communication. Through prayer (talking with God), we are communicating with our God.

1 Peter 3:12 tells us, *"The eyes of the Lord are upon the righteous and His ears are attentive (open) to their prayers."* God is waiting, listening for the prayers of his people. Prayer is not to be a religious form with no power, it is to be effective and accurate, and it is to bring results. God watches over His Word to perform it. (Jeremiah 1:12).

Prayer that brings results must then be based on God's Word.

"For what God speaks is alive and full of power, making it active, operative, energising and effective, it is sharper than any two-edged sword, penetrating to the dividing line of the breath, of life (soul) and the (immortal) spirit, and of the joints and marrow (that is to the deepest parts of our nature), exposing and

sifting and analysing and judging the very thoughts and purposes of the heart." (Hebrews 4:12 Amplified Version).

Prayer is this living Word in our mouth. Our mouth must speak forth faith, for faith is what pleases God. (Hebrews 11:6). When we pray, we hold up His Word to Him, and our Father watches over His Word to perform it.

God's Word is our contact with Him. We put Him in remembrance of His Word (Isaiah 43:26 Old Testament) placing a demand on His ability in the name of the Lord Jesus. We remind Him that He supplies all our needs according to His riches in glory by Christ Jesus (Philippians 4:19). That Word does not return to Him void, that is, without producing any effect, but it shall accomplish that which He pleases and purposes, and it shall prosper in the thing where unto He sent it. (Isaiah 55:11 Old Testament).

Here we can see, it is God's will that His Word (His will) be carried out in the earth. God did not leave us without His thoughts and His ways, for we have His Word, His bond. God instructs us to call upon Him and He will answer and show us great and mighty things. (Jeremiah 33:3 Old Testament). Prayer then is to be exciting. It takes someone to pray, God moves as we pray in faith, believing. He tells us to come believing to the throne of grace and obtain mercy and find grace to help in time of need. (Hebrews 4:16).

Let's read from the Book of Ephesians 6:10-18, *"Finally, my brethren, be strong in the Lord, and in the power of His might. Put on the whole armour of*

God, that ye may be able to stand against the wiles of the devil. For we wrestle not against flesh and blood, but against principalities, against powers, against the rulers of the darkness of this world, against spiritual wickedness in high places. Wherefore, take unto you the whole armour of God, that ye may be able to withstand in the evil day, and having done all, to stand. Stand therefore, having your loins girt about with truth, and having on the breastplate of righteousness; And your feet shod with the preparation of the gospel of peace; Above all, taking the shield of faith, wherewith ye shall be able to quench all the fiery darts of the wicked. And take the helmet of salvation, and sword of the Spirit, which is the Word of God. Praying always with all prayer, and supplication in the Spirit, and watching thereunto with all perseverance and supplication for all saints."

Using the Word in prayer is not taking it out of context, for His Word in us is the key to answered prayer. The prayer armour we read about here is for every believer, every part of the body of Christ, who will put it on and walk in it. 2 Corinthians 10:4 tells us that the weapons of our warfare are not carnal, but are mighty through God to the pulling down of strongholds of our enemy, Satan, the god of this world, and his demonic forces.

So then, as we can see here from this scripture in the Book of Ephesians Chapter 6, spiritual warfare takes place in prayer.

There are many different kinds of prayer, such as the prayer of thanksgiving and praise, prayer of dedication and worship, and the prayer that changes things and circumstances around us. All prayer involves time and fellowship with the Father. In Ephesians 6:18, we are instructed to take the sword of the Spirit, which is the Word of God, and pray at all times, on every occasion in every season, with all manner (that is different kinds) of prayers in the spirit, watching with all perseverance and supplication for all saints.

Prayer must be the foundation of every Christian's walk with God. Any failures in our life are often prayer failures. Our Father has not left us helpless. Not only has He given us His Word, but He has also given us His Holy Spirit to help our infirmities (our inabilities to produce results) when we know not how to pray as we ought (Romans 8:26).

Praise God! Our Father has provided His people with every possible avenue to ensure their complete and total victory in this life in the name of our Lord Jesus (1 John 5:3-5).

We pray to the Father, in the name of Jesus, through the Holy Spirit according to the Word!

Using God's Word on purpose, specifically in prayer, is one means of prayer, and it is the most effective and accurate means. Jesus said, *"The words that I have been speaking to you are spirit and life"* (John 6:63).

When Jesus faced Satan in the wilderness, He said, *"It is written... it is written... it is written."* We are to live, be upheld, and sustained by every Word that proceeds from the mouth of God (Matthew 4:4).

James, by the Spirit, admonishes that we do not have because we do not ask. We ask and receive not because we ask amiss (James 4:2 3). We must heed that admonishment now for we are to become experts in prayer rightly dividing the Word of Truth (2 Timothy 2:15). Using the Word is not taking it out of context, for His Word in us is the key to answered prayer that brings results. He is able to do exceedingly, abundantly above all we ask or think, according to the power that works in us. (Ephesians 3:20). The power lies within God's Word. It is anointed by the Holy Spirit. The Spirit of God does not lead us apart from the Word for the Word is of the Spirit of God. We apply that Word personally to ourselves and to others - not adding to or taking from it - in the name of Jesus. We apply the Word to the now - to those things, circumstances, and situations facing each of us now.

Paul was very specific and definite in his praying. The first chapter of Ephesians, Philippians, Colossians, and 2 Thessalonians are examples of how Paul prayed for believers. There are numerous others. Search them out. Paul wrote under the inspiration of the Holy Spirit. We can use these Spirit-given prayers today!

In 2 Corinthians 1:11, 2 Corinthians 9:14, and Philippians 1:4, we see examples of how believers prayed one for another - putting others first in their prayer life with joy. Our faith does work by love (Galatians 5:6). We grow spiritually as we reach out to help others - praying for and with them and holding out to them the Word of Life (Philippians 2:16).

(Joshua 1:8 Old Testament), We meditate on the Word day and night, do according to all that is written, and then shall we make our way prosperous and have good success. We are to attend to God's Word, submit to His sayings, keep them in the centre of our hearts. Prayer does not cause faith to work, but faith causes prayer to work. Therefore, any prayer problem is a problem of doubt -doubting the integrity of the Word and of the ability of God to stand behind His promises or the statements of fact in the Word.

We can spend fruitless hours in prayer if our hearts are not prepared beforehand. Preparation of the heart, the spirit, comes from meditation in the Father's Word, meditating on what we are in Christ, what He is to us, and what the Holy Spirit can mean to us as we become God-inside minded, as God told Joshua and put away contrary talk. (Proverbs 4:20-24).

The Word of God is likened unto seed in the Bible in Mark Chapter 4, so then we should seed every prayer with God's Word, then as we pray, what we are actually doing is holding God's Word before Him. We are confessing before our Father what He says belongs to us.

Those seeds (words) that we pray bear fruit. It is the law of Genesis. Every seed bears fruit after its own kind. As we pray, we expect God's divine intervention into the situation, while we make a choice not to look at the things that are seen, but at the things that are unseen, for the things that are seen are subject to change. Prayer based on the Word rises above the senses, contacts the Author of the Word, and sets His spiritual laws into motion. It is not just saying prayers that get results, but it is spending time fellowshipping with the Father, learning His wisdom, drawing on His strength, being filled with His peace and living in His love, that will bring results to our prayers.

> *"And in that day ye shall ask me nothing. Truly, Truly, I say unto you, 'Whatsoever ye shall ask the Father in My name, He will give it to you. Before now have ye asked nothing in My name; ask, and ye shall receive, that your joy may be full."* (John 16:23,24).

Prayer Must be Prayed in the Name of Jesus

> *"And his name through faith in his name hath made this man strong, whom you see and know: yes, the faith which is by him hath given him this perfect soundness in the presence of you all."* (Acts 3:16).

Here we can see it was His name and faith being released in and through that name, that gave the man his strength to walk. The healing manifested through the prayer, prayed in the powerful name of Jesus.

> *"And Jesus came and spake unto them, saying, All power is given unto me in heaven and in the earth. Go you therefore, and teach all nations, baptizing them in the name of the Father, and of the Son, and of the Holy Ghost: Teaching them to observe all things whatsoever I have commanded you: and, lo, I am with you always, even unto the end of the world. Amen."* (Matthew 28:18-20).

Jesus has all authority and He has given us the power of attorney to use that authority in His Name.

PRAYER REVISION

1. From what you have learnt, give a simple definition for prayer.

   ....

   ....

2. Write out and memorize James 5:16.

   ....

   ....

3. Write out and memorize 1 Peter 3:12.

   ....

   ....

4. Prayer should always be based on the Word of God to get results. *True or False*

5. Write out and memorize John 1:12.

   ....

   ....

   ....

6. Read Ephesians 6:10-18, list the armour of God that is at our disposal.

....

....

7. Prayer is one of the main foundations of a successful Christian walk.   *True or False*

8. Many failures we face as Christians are often prayer failures.   *True or False*

9. The Word of God in Mark Chapter 4 is likened unto seed, therefore we should seed every prayer with the Word of God.   *True or False*

10. According to the Law of Genesis Chapter 1, every seed bears fruit after its own kind.   *True or False*

11. From Acts 3:16, prayer must be prayed in who's name?

....

Chapter Eight

GOD'S WORD MUST BE CONFESSED

What a person says with his mouth can either release or negate (cancel out) what he believes in his heart. Not only does God desire His children to believe His Word, but also to speak and obey His Word. Jesus said "out of the abundance of the heart the mouth speaketh" (Matthew 12:34). Our mouths actually reveal what is in our hearts. Jesus explained the connection between the mouth and heart in this way:

> *"A good man out of the good treasure of the heart bringeth forth good things: and an evil man out of the evil treasure bringeth forth evil things. But I say unto you, that every idle word that men shall speak, they shall give account thereof in the day of judgment. For by thy words thou shalt be justified, and by thy words thou shalt be condemned"* (Matthew 12:35-37).

It does not take long to realize that Jesus believes that what we say is important. Our words will either justify or condemn us. There will be an account given of the words spoken by our mouth. If they are not according to the truth of God's Word, they will be idle, meaningless, and often times, very destructive.

Death and Life in the Tongue

"Death and life are in the power of the tongue: and they that love it shall eat the fruit thereof." (Proverbs 18:21 in the Old Testament).

This is practically the same thing Jesus said. The tongue can either work for us or against us. It is never a neutral force because it is usually speaking words of life or words of death. The words a man speaks create the blessings or curses that come his way in life. It is definitely God's desire to bless His children. But we must believe, speak, and obey God's Word BEFORE we can receive God's blessings.

"Thou art snared with the words of thy mouth, thou art taken with the words of thy mouth" (Proverbs 6:2).

The words we speak determine the life we enjoy. The reason is that our mouth is a revealer of the beliefs in our heart. If heart and mouth both get in accord with God's Word, then the blessings of God's Word begin to be tapped.

"A man's belly shall be satisfied with the fruit of his mouth; and with the increase of his lips shall he be filled." (Proverbs 18:20)

Salvation, blessing, prosperity, victory, and joy are all promised in God's Word. The man who receives them is the one who believes the promise and begins to confess it with his mouth.

Believe and Confess

*"But what saith it? The Word is nigh thee, even in thy **MOUTH**, and in thy **HEART:** that is the **WORD OF FAITH**, which we preach; that if thou shalt **CONFESS WITH THY MOUTH** the Lord Jesus, and shalt **BELIEVE IN THINE HEART** that God hath raised him from the dead, thou shalt be saved. For with the **HEART** man **BELIEVETH** unto righteousness; and with the **MOUTH CONFESSION** is made unto salvation"* (Romans 10:8-10).

Paul preached the word of faith to the people in Rome. He told them that this Word is in two places: in their heart to believe, and in their mouth to confess. This Scripture tells us that confession is part of salvation, just as believing is part of salvation.

Whenever we hear the good news of God's Word, it is up to us to believe and confess it personally. Thus we begin the important process of both hearing and doing the Word. Jesus equated this to a man building his house upon the rock. (Matthew 7:24).

Keep the Word in Your Mouth

God has given us a formula for success as we go about our daily routine of living. It is a message that He spoke first to Joshua concerning his success as a leader of Israel.

> *"This book of the law shall not depart out of thy mouth; but thou shalt meditate therein day and night, that thou mayest observe to do according to all that is written therein: for then thou shalt make thy way prosperous, and then thou shalt have good success"* (Joshua 1:8 in the Old Testament).

The formula for success that God gave to Joshua was:
1. Keep the Word (book of the Law) in your mouth.
2. Meditate day and night in that Word.
3. Do what the Word says.

Notice that God said Joshua would make his own way prosperous by doing these things. He would not only have success, but it would be *"good success"*.

It is no wonder that David prayed to God,
> *"Let the words of my mouth, and the meditation of my heart be acceptable in Thy sight, O Lord, my Strength, and my Redeemer"* (Psalm 19:14 Old Testament).

David knew that his own success greatly depended upon his meditation and confession. He had experienced a tremendous victory as a teenager because of meditating God's Word and boldly speaking it forth in the face of Goliath (1 Samuel 17:45-50 Old Testament). Remember, he spoke words of faith **BEFORE** the giant fell. Anyone can shout after the victory is won, but it takes faith to shout **BEFORE** the walls fall (Joshua 6:16).

The important thing to remember in faith confession is that God's Word must be the foundation. We must know the truth and be convinced concerning God's will (2 Timothy 2:15). Then God will back our confession, because he is faithful to keep His Word (Numbers 23:19).

No Corrupt Communication

Begin to speak forth God's Word, believing He will bring it to pass. At the same time, stop speaking negative words that are contrary to the Word of God. In the beginning, this may seem a little strange, but it will become a tremendous blessing. Make a decision to say as David says, "Set a watch O Lord, before my mouth; keep the door of my lips" (Psalm 141:3 Old Testament).

Refrain from speaking anything evil, negative, critical, or idle. If I must say something, then I think first and speak about, *"whatsoever things are true, whatsoever things are honest, whatsoever things are just, whatsoever things are pure, whatsoever things are lovely, whatsoever things are of good report"* (Philippians 4:8).

Generally, a person cannot improve a situation by speaking negatively about it. Nor can he help someone by criticising them without love. But if a person speaks God's Word over the situation or person, he has released his faith and brought the power of the Lord on the scene.

"Let no corrupt communication proceed out of your mouth, but that which is good to the use of

edifying, that it may minister grace unto the hearers" (Ephesians 4:29).

Every time we speak, we hear ourselves and God hears us. By speaking the Words of life, we can minister to ourselves and to God, not to mention what it will do in the lives of others that hear our conversation.

Overcoming by the Word of our Testimony

Those that overcome Satan will be required to use the power of the spoken Word. It is the sword of the spirit in the Christian's armour (Ephesians 6:17). Jesus spoke the Word aloud directly to Satan in the wilderness (Matthew 4:1 11), thus giving a battle-plan to the Christian on how to defeat the devil. We can resist the devil with the Word and he will flee (James 4:7).

> *"And they overcame him by the blood of the lamb, and by the word of their testimony; and they loved not their lives unto the death"* (Revelation 12:11).

The blood of Jesus cleanses us from all sin and frees us from all condemnation from Satan (1 John 1:7, Romans 8:1). The word of our testimony is the sword that puts Satan to flight. It is the Word of God coming from our lips that produces an overcoming spirit in us.

Speak to the Mountain

Jesus said, "Have faith in God. For verily I say unto you, that whosoever shall say unto this mountain, Be thou removed, and be thou cast into the sea; and shall not doubt in his heart, but shall believe that those things which he saith shall come to pass; he shall have whatsoever he saith" (Mark 11:22-23).

Jesus said the person who believes in his heart what he says with his mouth, would have what he says. It is true we have the things we believe and speak. For instance, the person who believes he is going to get angry over a situation and then says, "I'm going to get mad," usually will get mad. This just seems to work in every area of life. The reason is because it is a spiritual law. It works whether we believe it or not. It is the same as the physical law of gravity - it works regardless of our attitude towards it.

If I believe God's Word is true for me, then I can begin to claim its promises by confessing them in my life. Faith requires me to speak them before I feel or see them.

If there is a mountain of a problem in my life, family, body, or finances, I must speak directly to the problem. As I speak, I must believe that what I say will come to pass. God says that what I say will become a visible reality in the natural world if I steadfastly hold to my confession of faith.

There is power in our mouth. The belief in our heart is released by faith out of our mouth. By believing, confessing, and acting on God's Word, we can receive salvation, healing, the Holy Spirit, righteousness, and a victorious abundant life. All of these are promised to the Christian and available by faith.

GOD'S WORD MUST BE CONFESSED
REVISION

1. You can negate or cancel out what you believe in your heart by speaking different things out of your mouth. *True or False*

2. God wants us not just to believe his Word, but also to speak it.   *True or False*

3. Death and Life are in the power of your own tongue. *True or False*

4. Write out and memorise Proverbs 18:21.

   ....

   ....

5. According to Matthew 12:35-37, our words either justify us or condemn us.   *True or False*

6. Write out and memorise Proverbs 6:2.

   ....

   ....

   ....

7. Write out and memorise Romans 10:8-10.

   ....

   ....

   ....

8. Study Joshua 1:8. What are the three main things God gave Joshua in the formula for success:

   1. ....
   2. ....
   3. ....

9. God told Joshua that by following this formula for success as listed here in Joshua 1:8, that Joshua would be able to make his own way prosperous.
   True or False

10. Write out and memorise Psalm 19:14.

    ....

    ....

    ....

11. It takes faith to shout victory before the battle is fought.
    True or False

12. Write out your own brief understanding of Mark 11:22-23.

....

....

....

Chapter Nine

CONFESSIONS FOR VICTORY

"Death and life are in the power of the tongue, and they that love it will eat the fruit thereof".
(Proverbs 18:21 Old Testament).

From the above scripture, we can see how powerful the words of our mouth are. With them, we have the choice to speak death or life into any situation that faces us.

God's plan is victory for every human being. You were created to have dominion on the earth. Jesus Christ regained the authority that Adam, the first man, had lost. You were born again to be a winner, to be triumphant.

God has plans for your life, beyond your wildest dreams. Make a decision today to choose life. God has absolute victory for you. Don't make wrong confessions, agree with God, and agree with His Word. Speak life, speak God's Word, confess daily God's Word over your life, your family and anything else that concerns you. You are what God says you are, you can do what God says you can do.

The following list is a few of the precious promises from God's Word. You can confess boldly every day about any situation that may arise in your life.

Taken from Don Gossett's 'Never Again List".
Used with permission.

NEVER AGAIN CONFESS DEFEAT FOR:
"God ... always causeth us to triumph in Christ..." (2 Corinthians 2:14).

NEVER AGAIN CONFESS BONDAGE FOR:
"Where the Spirit of the Lord, there is liberty" (2 Corinthians 3:17).

NEVER AGAIN CONFESS SICKNESS FOR:
"With his stripes, we are healed" (Isaiah 53:5).
"He Himself took our infirmities, and bore our sicknesses" (Matthew 8:17).

NEVER AGAIN CONFESS FEAR FOR:
"God hath not given us the spirit of fear; but of power, and of love, and of a sound mind" (2 Timothy 1:7).

NEVER AGAIN CONFESS, I CAN'T FOR:
"I can do all things through Christ which strengtheneth me" (Philippians 4:13).

NEVER AGAIN CONFESS DOUBT AND LACK OF FAITH FOR:
"God hath dealt to every man the measure of faith" (Romans 12:3).

NEVER AGAIN CONFESS WEAKNESS FOR:
"The Lord is the strength of my life..." (Psalm 27:1 Old Testament).
"The people that do know their God shall be strong, and do exploits" (Daniel 11:32 Old Testament).

NEVER AGAIN CONFESS SATAN'S SUPREMACY OVER YOUR LIFE FOR:
"Greater is He that is in you, than he that is in the world" (1 John 4:4).

NEVER AGAIN CONFESS A LACK OF WISDOM FOR:
"But of him are ye in Christ Jesus, who of God is made unto us wisdom..." (1 Corinthians 1:30).

NEVER AGAIN CONFESS FEELINGS OF GUILT FOR:
"There is therefore now no condemnation to them which are in Christ Jesus" (Romans 8:1).
"As far as the east is from the west, so far hath he removed our transgressions from us" (Psalm 103:12 Old Testament).

NEVER AGAIN CONFESS WORRY FOR:
"*Casting all your care upon him; for he careth for you*" (1 Peter 5:7).

NEVER AGAIN CONFESS DISCONTENT FOR:
"*For I have learned, in whatsoever state I am, therewith to be content*" (Philippians 4:11).

NEVER AGAIN CONFESS LONELINESS FOR JESUS SAID:
"*I will never leave thee, nor forsake thee*" *(Hebrews 13:5).* "*Lo, I am with you always, even unto the end of the world*" (Matthew 28:20).

NEVER AGAIN CONFESS A FEAR OF THE FUTURE FOR:
"*Eye hath not seen, nor ear heard, neither have entered into the heart of man, the things which God hath prepared for them that love Him. But God hath revealed them unto us by his Spirit...*" (1 Corinthians 2:9,10).

NEVER AGAIN CONFESS AN INABILITY TO CONQUER SIN IN YOUR LIFE FOR:
"*For the law of the Spirit of life in Christ Jesus hath made me free from the law of sin and death*" (Romans 8:2).

NEVER AGAIN CONFESS FRUSTRATION FOR:
"Thou wilt keep him in perfect peace, whose mind is stayed on thee" (Isaiah 26:3 Old Testament).

NEVER AGAIN CONFESS CONFUSION FOR:
"Now we have received, not the spirit of the world, but the spirit which is of God; that we might know the things that are freely given to us of God"
(1 Corinthians 2:12).

"For God is not the author of confusion, but of peace"
(1 Corinthians 14:33).

NEVER AGAIN CONFESS FAILURE FOR:
"Nay, in all these things we are more than conquerors through Him that loved us" (Romans 8:37).

Faith is an Act

Kenneth E. Hagin would always say "Faith is an act." I like to say, "The Word works, when you work the Word."

If we want to realise the mighty power of faith contained in the Word of God and experience its benefits, then we must be doers of the Word and not hearers only. (James 1:22). For it is in doing of God's Word that we are blessed. As we put the promises to work through the power of confession, we will reap the benefits in our lives, family and business.

CONFESSIONS FOR VICTORY
REVISION

1. You were created by God to reign and rule in this life by Jesus Christ.   *True or False*

2. You were born again to win and be successful in life. *True or False*

3. The rest of your homework for this lesson is to l earn these powerful faith confessions and scriptures. They are precious promises in God's Word, designed by God to build faith in you and give you victory. Speak them every morning for the next two weeks and as you say them personalise them; e.g. Romans 8:37, *"I am more than a conqueror through Him that loves me."*

CHAPTER TEN

FAITH

᎚   ᎙

Faith is the most crucial subject in the bible, because faith gives us access to all the promises of God, including salvation.

Paul writes in Romans 1:16-17 that he is *"not ashamed of the Gospel of Christ, for it is the power of God to salvation to everyone who believes, to the Jew first and also to the Greek. For therein is the righteousness of God revealed from faith to faith, as it is written, the just shall live by faith."* We are not only saved by faith and trust in God's Word, but from these scriptures, we can clearly see, that God expects us as believers to live by faith.

What is Faith?

Very simply, we could say that faith is having trust and confidence in God, or trust and confidence in the Word of God. Hebrews 11:1 tells us, *"Now faith is the substance of things hoped for, the evidence of things not seen."* Faith is always in the present tense. It believes now, it receives now and acts now. It simply believes that God is able. God can do what He promised He would do. Faith believes and expects He will do it for us. Faith receives now!

<u>Faith is Always Now!</u>

One of the great differences between faith and hope is the tense. Hope is usually concerned with the future, where faith is most often concerned with the present. Sometimes we hear people say they are stepping out in faith in a new venture, but usually, they really do not know what is going to happen or what the future holds. They feel the urge to try something new and to take a stab at it, but that is not the faith we are talking about in Hebrews 11:1. Bible faith does not operate this way. True faith in God's Word has power, and when we step out in this kind of faith, we are standing on solid rock - the solid rock of God's unchanging, eternal Word, the same substance that God used when He created the heavens and the earth.

> Hebrews 11:3 says, *"Through faith we understand that the worlds were framed by the Word of God, so that things which are seen were not made of things which do appear."*

<u>Hope is Not Faith</u>

We may hope for something for years - as long as we continue hoping, it will just be beyond us, but there are, on the other hand, many good things, many blessings, we can bring into our lives by faith in God and His unchanging Word.

For instance, salvation, or eternal life, is a good thing to hope for, but if we want to be saved, we need to put substance to our hope and receive Christ by faith right now. Although we do not see Jesus, although we may not feel any different, we are still saved, if we have put our faith in Jesus Christ. Although there may be no physical evidence for our faith, we do have sufficient evidence in God's Word. God is a witness; He will never lie. If we take God at His Word, that Word will stand good in the trial.

How Do We Get Faith?

*"So then **FAITH COMETH BY HEARING**, and hearing by the Word of God"* (Romans 10:17). The best way to get faith is to hear the Word of God. It is important for us not only to hear it with our ears but also with our hearts. To hear God's Word in our hearts requires openness and hunger for God's message.

I suggest reading the Bible aloud, particularly the New Testament. Say the scriptures to yourselves. Insert your own name where the message is personal. Make a list of the promises God's Word has for you. By faith, believe, receive, and confess them daily. Faith will grow as we continually hear God's Word.

Who Can Have Faith?

*".... God hath dealt to **EVERY MAN** the measure of faith"* (Romans 12:3).

Paul is writing to the Christians in Rome. God has dealt to every Christian the measure of faith. But we also have faith to be saved before we are Christians. The Bible says *"whosoever will"* (Revelation 22:17) can be saved. Evidently, any person who hears God's Word and will act on it can exercise faith. That includes all who will **HEAR** and **OBEY** God's Word - saved or in the process of being saved.

People who do not hear God's Word or will not obey it do not have the God-kind of faith. Faith requires hearing and obeying.

> *"And that we may be delivered from unreasonable and wicked men: for **ALL MEN HAVE NOT FAITH**"* (2 Thessalonians 3:2).

So then anybody who is prepared to hear and study God's Word and act on it, can have faith and increase their faith. Faith is like a muscle; the more you use it, the stronger it will grow.

Faith Acts on God's Word

God has spread a table before us filled with bountiful blessings. Naturally speaking, if someone sets a beautiful table of food before us, we know what to do with it. We do not sit wishing and hoping that we could have some of that food. We do not complain to our host that we do not have enough. Neither do we get mad and upset if someone else at the table gets a big helping of mashed potatoes. We begin to help ourselves to the food. It has been set before us to eat and be filled. There is probably more in the kitchen if we empty the serving bowls. We know that everyone at the table has equal rights and privileges to get their portion of each dish.

Know God's Word is the same. God has made ample provision for every need in our lives. He promises a full, abundant supply. It is all ours for the asking. God just wants us to believe His Word and take what has been set before us. It does not offend God for us to take all we need. Any hostess is disappointed if she discovers one of her guests did not get enough. She wants each one to be satisfied. God is certainly the Almighty Creator, but He has chosen to set a table for us. What we receive from Him will come as a result of our actively reaching out and claiming His promises.

> *"And Jesus answered and said unto him. 'What wilt thou that I should do unto thee?' And the blind man said unto Him, 'Lord, that I might receive my sight.' Jesus said unto him, 'Go thy way; thy faith hath made thee whole.' And immediately he received his sight and followed Jesus in the way"* (Mark 10:51-52).

Faith is Not a Feeling

Sometimes people base their spiritual experiences on feelings and emotions. Problems arise when feelings and emotions change. If they have not been grounded in the Word of God, doubt will arise as to whether or not the experience was genuine. For faith to be consistent, it must be based on something with more stability than our feelings.

No person is saved because he feels saved. He is saved because he has put on his faith in God's Word and acted on it. He may feel great today, tired tomorrow, and lonely next week, but Hallelujah! God's Word is going to say the same thing yesterday, today and forever (Hebrews 13:8).

Feelings are influenced by what we see, what we read, and what we hear. Everyone is exposed to things that are not consistent with God's Word. If these things control our feeling and our feelings control our faith, we can be Christians yet controlled by Satan's devices.

Our faith must be controlled by God's Word, not by what we feel, not by what circumstances look like, and not by what others tell us. *"For we walk by faith, not by sight"* (2 Corinthians 5:7). Our eyes, ears, heart, and mouth should be tuned to God's Word.

> *"While we look not at the things which are seen, but at the things which are not seen, for the things which are seen are temporal; but the things which are not seen are eternal"* (2 Corinthians 4:18).

God's Word is eternal. Our spiritual eyes must be focused on God (Who is unseen) by looking at His Word.

Faith is Available to Everyone

I encourage you today to study God's Word to find precious promises and blessings He has for you, and then reach out and receive them into your life by faith. Claim them by faith as your very own and praise and thank God for them. (Mark 11:22, 23 and 24).

FAITH REVISION

1. Write out and memorise Romans 1:16,17.

   ....

   ....

   ....

2. Write out and memorise Hebrews 11:1.

   ....

   ....

   ....

3. Write out and memorise Hebrews 11:3.

   ....

   ....

   ....

4. Write out and memorise Romans 10:17.

   ....

   ....

   ....

5. Faith is an act. It's acting on the Word of God.
   True or False

6. Faith is always in the present time.   *True or False*

7. Faith is not based on feelings.   *True or False*

8. Faith is trust in the Word of God, having confidence in God and His Word.   *True or False.*

CHAPTER ELEVEN

ABUNDANT VICTORIOUS LIFE

Jesus said in the scriptures, that He has come to give us life and that life more abundantly. (John 10:10). This life of God is superior in quality and overflowing in quantity. It's God's life manifested in the believer by the Spirit of God, through His Word.

God has made provision for every Christian to live this life in absolute victory and abundance. Just because others may not be experiencing victory in their lives does not mean that God has not provided it. He has done everything in His power to give His children the authority and provision needed to live triumphantly on this earth.

This is the Victory - OUR FAITH

"For whatsoever is born of God overcometh the world: and this is the victory that overcometh the world, even our faith. Who is he that overcometh the world; but he that believeth that Jesus is the Son of God?" (1 John 5:4 5).

God does not give victory over the world just to a select few. He has given overcoming victory to every person that is born again. It is a gift of God, just as salvation is a gift from God. It cannot be purchased, earned or merited by good works or deeds. It can only be received by faith, which is why the verse says the victory is in our faith - our believing, receiving, confessing, and doing the Word of God.

Victory is a Gift

> *"But thanks be to God, which giveth us the victory through our Lord Jesus Christ"* (1 Corinthians 15:57).

No man can glory in his victory in this life. All credit goes to God. He deserves our thanksgiving. He has given to us victory over Satan, sin, sickness and fear. When Jesus arose triumphantly from the grave, He won a complete victory over all the forces of darkness. He did it for us.

It was mankind that needed victory. So Jesus was made in the likeness of men (Philippians 2:7). He was our substitute. His victory was our victory.

> *"Now thanks be unto God, which always causeth us to triumph in Christ, and maketh manifest the savour of His knowledge by us in every place"* (2 Corinthians 2:14).

Triumph in Christ does not have to be an occasional experience. God has made it possible for us to ALWAYS be triumphant in Him no matter what comes, because He does not change.

More Than Conquerors

"Nay, in all these things we are more than conquerors through Him that loved us" (Romans 8:37).

Amazing! Not just a conqueror, but **MORE** than a conqueror. That means more than a conqueror over every obstacle, every mountain, and every adversity the enemy would try and bring against us.

Notice again that it is *"through Him"* that we are more than conquerors. There can be no victory, no conquering spirit, apart from a vital union with our Lord Jesus Christ. This comes through fellowship with the Father, Son and Holy Spirit in prayer and meditation of the Word.

All Things are Possible

The apostle Paul was human just like anyone else. One reason he was able to accomplish all that he did was his understanding of God's ability inside him. The bible says, *"It is Christ in us, the hope of glory"* (Colossians 1:27). He did not boast of his own strength and power, but he boasted of God's ability. He realised that true humility means total dependence upon God for everything. He believed the Word that had been revealed to him, and he acted upon it. Because of this, he was able to say, *"I can do all things through Christ which strengtheneth me"* (Philippians 4.13).

The same Jesus who enabled Paul to do all things lives in every born again believer. Each one has the privilege of boldly declaring, *"I can do all things through Christ which strengtheneth me."* It is HIS strength, HIS power, HIS ability. All we have to do is rely upon Him, knowing that whatever He gives us to do, we can do through Jesus.

Greater is He

"You are of God, little children, and have overcome them: because greater is He that is in you, than he that is in the world" (1 John 4:4).

This message is to the child of God. Every born again believer has the ability to overcome the spirits of Antichrist that are in the world. As far as God is concerned, we will never have victory until we believe that victory was obtained through Christ. It is a past tense victory. John says that the believer "has overcome" them. The reason, he explains, is quite simple. The greater one, Jesus, lives in the believer. Jesus is greater than the devil, who is in the world. Nothing the devil might try to bring against the Christian can be greater than Jesus. Therefore, the saved person can reckon that he is an overcomer because the One who overcame everything, lives inside him. Of course, the believer must overcome obstacles daily by acting on God's Word.

Powerful Weapons

"Wherefore take unto you the whole armour of God, that you may be able to withstand in the evil day, and

having done all, to stand. Stand therefore, having your loins girt about with **TRUTH**, *and having on the* **BREASTPLATE OF RIGHTEOUSNESS;** *And your feet shod with the preparation of the* **GOSPEL OF PEACE;** *Above all, taking the* **SHIELD OF FAITH,** *wherewith you shall be able to quench all the fiery darts of the wicked. And take the* **HELMET OF SALVATION,** *and the* **SWORD OF THE SPIRIT,** *which is the* **WORD OF GOD:** *Praying always with all* **PRAYER** *and* **SUPPLICATION** *in the* **SPIRIT,** *and watching thereunto with all perseverance and supplication for all saints"* (Ephesians 6:13-18).

There is definitely a battle to wage with the evil powers. But God has given us all the armour needed. He has given us weapons that no power of Satan can stop. Our command is to *"put on the whole armour of God"* (Ephesians 6:10). Not even the gates of hell can stand against the fully armed church of the Lord Jesus Christ (Matthew 16:18).

"For the weapons of our warfare are not carnal, but mighty through God to the pulling down of strongholds; Casting down imaginations and every high thing that exalteth itself against the knowledge of God, and bringing into captivity every thought to the obedience of Christ" (2 Corinthians 10:4-5).

The weapons God has provided, give us the authority to pull down every fortress that Satan would try to build against us. He is powerless in the face of God's armour and weapons.

Joint Heirs with Christ

Jesus came to restore the relationship and fellowship between God and man. His desire is for man to enjoy the full privileges of being part of God's family. One of my favourite verses in the bible is John 10:10. The source of stealing, killing and destruction is not God, but Satan, Jesus said, *"The thief cometh not, but for to steal, and to kill and to destroy: I have come that they might have life, and that they might have it more abundantly"* (John 10:10).

Abundant life! That is abundant life in every part of man's existence - spiritual, mental, physical, financial. This includes the home, family, work and school.

> *"The Spirit itself beareth witness with our spirit, that we are the children of God: And if children, then heirs; heirs of God, and joint heirs with Christ; if so be that we suffer with him, that we may be also glorified together"* (Romans 8:16-17).

We can enjoy the blessings of being a joint-heir with Christ if we will steadfastly hold to the Word of God. Not only must we be true to the Word, but also gladly bear the reproaches of the ungodly that come as a result of living as a child of the King. It is a joy, not a burden!

Prospering in Every Area of Life

God's will is for us to prosper in every area of life. A person could be a loyal and sincere Christian without prospering in all the areas of life. One could even be very successful in some areas without claiming all of God's promises. But why should any Christian not want all God has provided? All the provisions of God are needed in order to be *"fruitful in every good work"* (Colossians 1:10).

Freely Given All Things

"He that spared not his own Son, but delivered him up for us all, how shall He not with Him also freely give us all things?" (Romans 8:32).

If God gave us the most priceless possession He had, His son, why would He withhold from us anything of less value? It is His desire to give us everything (all things) we need in this life and the life to come. We will be involved in working and labouring in various ways. But it will be God who works through these different means to *"freely give us all things."*

Blessed With Every Spiritual Blessing

"Blessed be the God and Father of our Lord Jesus Christ, who has blessed us with all spiritual blessings in heavenly places in Christ" (Ephesians 1:3).

God has already blessed us with all the spiritual blessings we can handle on this earth. The blessings are available. Possibly *"...you have not, because you ask not"*, or, *"you ask, and receive not, because you ask amiss, that you may consume it upon your lusts"* (James 4:3).

The primary reason in asking for God's blessings should be to share them with others. When our needs are met, we have an abundance to share with those around us.

God's Intent for Us

"Beloved, I wish above all things that thou mayest prosper and be in health, even as thy soul prospereth" (3 John 2).

The first place we are to prosper is in our spiritual lives. As the *"law of the Spirit of life in Christ Jesus"* begins to rule in our hearts, it will *"set us free from the laws of sin and death"* that would try to enslave us mentally, physically, spiritually and financially (Romans 8:2).

"But my God shall supply all your need according to his riches in glory by Christ Jesus" (Philippians 4:19).

God is our source. He supplies our need. The basis for that supply is all of the riches in glory of Christ Jesus. The supply is unlimited. As we seek first the kingdom of God and His righteousness, all these things shall be added unto us (Matthew 6:33).

Abounding to Every Good Work

As we give ourselves totally to God and His kingdom, we know that God will gladly give us all of His life. The Christian that gives his best to God and expects God's best, becomes extremely useful in the work of the kingdom.

"And God is able to make all grace abound toward you; that ye always having all sufficiency in all things, may abound to every good work" (2 Corinthians 9:8).

The most important thing to remember in living the abundant life is: BE A GIVER - First to God, then to our fellow man. God will see to it that we abound in everything we do. He will supply all the needs and make His grace abound in us, so that we will never lack in any good work to which He calls us.

"Give, and it shall be given unto you; good measure, pressed down, and shaken together, and running over, shall men give into your bosom. For with the same measure that ye mete withal it shall be measured to you again" (Luke 6:38).

God always multiplies back to us more than we give. It is the law of seed time and harvest. (Genesis 8:22).

ABUNDANT VICTORIOUS LIFE REVISION

1. Write out and memorise 1 John 5:4-5.

   ....

   ....

   ....

2. Write out and memorise Romans 8:37.

   ....

   ....

   ....

3. Write out and memorise Philippians 4:13.

   ....

   ....

   ....

4. Write out and memorise 1 John 4:4.

   ....

   ....

   ....

5. The weapons God has provided give us the authority to pull down every fortress that Satan would try to build against us.   *True or False*

6. God will not withhold any good thing from him or her that walks uprightly.   *True or False*

7. Fill in the blanks: Philippians 4:19 "But my God .... supply .... your needs according to His .... in glory by ....

8. John 10:10: The thief cometh not, but for to steal, kill and to destroy, I have come that they may have .... and that they might have it more ....

9. In your own words, describe what it was to have abundant life in Christ.

   ....

   ....

   ....

10. In your own words, describe what 3 John 2 means to you.

....

....

....

CHAPTER TWELVE

HEALING

God is a Healer

God revealed Himself to the people of Israel as a healer-God. Jehovah Rapha. He promised to keep disease from them if they would obey His Word.

> *"If thou wilt diligently hearken to the voice of the Lord thy God, and wilt do that which is right in His sight, and wilt give ear to His commandments, and keep all His statutes, I will put none of these diseases upon thee, which I have brought upon the Egyptians; for I am the Lord that healeth thee."* (Exodus 15:26 Old Testament.)

Healing - One of God's Benefits

God is a Father to His children. Because of His compassion for those He loves, He has made provision for their healing. This is one of the benefits of having a loving heavenly Father who cares for our every need.

> *"Bless the Lord. O my soul, and forget not all His benefits: Who forgiveth all thine iniquities; who healeth all thy diseases".* (Psalms 103:2,3 Old Testament).

Notice that forgiveness is one of God's benefits. They are both placed together in this passage of scripture. God is concerned about both our spiritual healing and our physical healing.

Messiah Suffers for Our Healing

The prophet Isaiah wrote about the One who was to suffer, the Messiah or Redeemer of Israel. He was writing about Jesus taking our punishment for our sins. Jesus suffered for us in every way we deserved to suffer. Physically, mentally, spiritually. He did it in order that we might not have to suffer these things. He was our substitute, our Saviour.

The four Gospel writers tell us what they **SAW** and **HEARD** about the suffering of Christ. On the other hand, Isaiah tells us what was **REVEALED** to him by the Spirit of God concerning Christ's sufferings.

> *"Surely He hath borne our griefs and carried our sorrows; yet we did esteem Him stricken, smitten of God, and afflicted. But He was wounded for our transgressions, He was bruised for our iniquities; the chastisement of our peace was upon Him; and **WITH HIS STRIPES WE ARE HEALED**. All*

we like sheep have gone astray; we have turned every one to his own way; and the Lord hath laid on Him the iniquity of us all" (Isaiah 53:4-6 Old Testament).

The two words *"griefs"* and *"sorrows"* in the first phrase of the passage could equally be translated sicknesses and pains. This will be clearer after reading Matthew 8:16-17. From these three verses, we see the variety of things Jesus suffered as He took our place and God's judgement for sin fell on Him.

He Took Our Infirmities and Bore Our Sicknesses

While Jesus walked the face of the earth, He ministered healing to every part of man. He cast out devils, healed the sick, forgave sin, and restored wholeness to those tormented by Satan. In recording these events, Matthew quoted from Isaiah 53:4 (Old Testament) concerning the substitutionary work of Christ.

"When the evening was come they brought unto Him many that were possessed with devils; and He cast out the spirits with His Word, and healed all that were sick; that it might be fulfilled which was spoken by Isaiah the prophet, saying, **HE HIMSELF TOOK OUR INFIRMITIES, AND BARE OUR SICKNESS"** *(*Matthew 8:16-17).

Not only did He take our infirmities and bare all our sicknesses on the cross, but also during His ministry, He relieved people of infirmities and sicknesses. He did this in relation to sins also. Not only did He take our sins on the cross, but He also forgave men of their sins before the crucifixion.

Healed by His Stripes

Peter was a man who witnessed the mock trial of Jesus. He was well acquainted with the happenings on Calvary. He wrote about the effects that Jesus' suffering would have on our lives. He mentions both the spiritual and the physical results of Christ's atonement.

> *"Who His own self bare our sins in His own body on the tree, that we, being dead to sins, should live unto righteousness:* **BY WHOSE STRIPES YE ARE HEALED"** 1 Peter 2:24.

The phrase *"by whose stripes ye are healed"* is a direct reference to Isaiah 53:5 in the Old Testament. You remember that Jesus was scourged or whipped before his crucifixion (Mark 15:15). The physical punishment that He took was for our healing, for *"with His stripes we are healed"* (Isaiah 53:5). All the punishment Jesus received before and during the crucifixion was for our healing - spirit, soul and body.

Satan is the Author of Sickness and Disease

Before Adam's sin in the garden, there was no sin or death on the earth. After his disobedience, sin and death with all of their evil companions (hatred, bitterness, jealously, sickness, disease, torment) entered into the world (Romans 5:12). Jesus was sent to re-establish the wholeness that man had before the fall. He was the Redeemer, the One sent to buy us back from the dominion of Satan. Jesus freed the people who were captive to Satan's devices. He healed the sick, delivered the oppressed, opened prison doors, and preached the Good News.

> "How God anointed Jesus of Nazareth with the Holy Spirit and with power: who went about doing good, and healing all that were oppressed of the devil: for God was with Him." (Acts 10:38).

This scripture, as well as all four gospels, clearly reveals that the devil oppresses people with sickness, and Jesus heals people who are sick. Never confuse these two. God desires an abundant life for us, and the devil wants to steal, to kill and to destroy. (John 10:10)

God Wants Us In Health

> "Beloved, I wish above all things that thou mayest prosper and be in health, even as thy soul prospereth" (3 John 2).

God is interested in our health, spiritually and physically. He wants our bodies to be just as free from Satan's influence as He does our hearts.

> "For ye are bought with a price: therefore glorify God in your body, and in your spirit, which are God's" (1 Corinthians 6:20).

Not only are we to live holy and pure lives in our body, but also it is possible for us to live in health. We have been bought with the blood of Christ. The price has been paid for spiritual and physical health.

Redeemed From the Curse

"Christ hath redeemed us from the curse of the law, being made a curse for us: for it is written, Cursed is every one that hangeth on a tree: That the blessing of Abraham might come on the Gentiles through Jesus Christ; that we might receive the promise of the Spirit through faith" (Galatians 3:13-14).

There was a curse pronounced upon those who would not keep God's laws (Deuteronomy 28:15-68). This curse generally included poverty, sickness, and death. Since all men were sinners, there was no man who could fully keep all God's laws (Romans 3:23).

Jesus entered the earth as a man and lived His life without sin. As he hung on the cross, He was actually made to be a curse for us, as our substitute. He took the curse we deserved. He took our poverty, our sickness, and our death (sin), so that we might receive the blessings God has promised to Abraham and those keeping His law. These include an abundant supply for every need in our lives (Deuteronomy 28:1-14 Old Testament).

In Acts 10:38 it tells us, *"How God anointed Jesus of Nazareth with the Holy Ghost and with power: who went about doing good, and healing all that were oppressed of the devil; for God was with him."*

Here we can see it was God who anointed Jesus with Holy Spirit power to do good and to heal. Jesus Christ came to save the lost and heal the sick. From the above scripture, we can also determine that sickness is an oppression sent by Satan from the kingdom of darkness.

Jesus is Still the Same

"Jesus Christ the same yesterday, and today, and forever" (Hebrews 13:8). The reason Jesus healed people was because of His compassion. He saw their needs and met them. He is still the same. His compassion has not stopped. He loves us just as much as He did those in the time of His earthly ministry. His power is not stopped just because He is no longer visibly in our midst. His power and effectiveness are even greater today because He can be present in all places at all times by His Spirit. *"His mercy endures forever"* (Psalm 136 in the Old Testament).

Prayer of Faith - Anointing with Oil

We know from the book of Acts that the healing ministry of Christ did not stop with His death and resurrection. It continued through the twelve disciples and the other believers (Mark 16:15-19).

There were numerous ways in which people received healing under Jesus' ministry. Today men can receive healing from the basis of numerous passages of scripture. These include: Mark 11:22-24; John 16:23-24; Matthew 18:18-20; Mark 16:18; James 5:14-15; Exodus 15:26; Psalms 103:3; 1 Peter 2:24; Matthew 8:16-17.

One important method is anointing with oil and praying the prayer of faith. It demonstrates to us that God's power can be ministered by believers, and this shows that healing did not end when Christ died or when the apostles died. Healing is still provided for us today.

"Is any sick among you? Let him call for the elders of the church, and let them pray over him, anointing him with oil in the name of the Lord: and the prayer of faith shall save the sick, and the Lord shall raise him up; and if he have committed sins, they shall be forgiven him" (James 5:14-15).

Laying on of Hands

Mark 16:15-18 states, *"And he said unto them, 'Go ye into all the world, and preach the gospel to every creature. He that believeth and is baptised shall be saved; but he that believeth not shall be damned. And these signs shall follow them that believe; In my name shall they cast out devils; they shall speak with new tongues; They shall take up serpents; and if they drink any deadly thing, it shall not hurt them; they shall lay hands on the sick, and they shall recover."*

Here in verse 18, we can see that Jesus said we can lay hands on the sick in His name, and they would recover or get well. Laying on of hands is another way by which healing can be received.

Casting Out Devils

Another way to heal the sick is by casting out a devil or spirit of infirmity. In verse 17 from the scripture above, Jesus said we have the power to cast devils in His name. This is any devil or spirit that is causing the curse to be active in your life. Many times the problems we are facing or going through are caused by devils or demons in the unseen realm of the spirit working through the curse of the law against us. Their destructive influences can be felt or seen in many ways.

In many of the different countries and places of the world that I have ministered, the Lord has instructed me to bind the forces first. On the prayer lines, I have prayed for hundreds of people over the years, taking authority over the spirit of infirmity in their life or body, the evil spirit that is empowering the sickness to destroy them. I have spoken to the spirit, casting it out and telling it to leave the person.

I have observed that as the spirit of infirmity and sickness has left, healing relief and deliverance has flowed back into their lives.

Now before I pray, I always bind the spirit of infirmity over the life of the person I am praying for, casting it out and telling it that it has no more power over that individual's life because of the shed blood and authority of the name of Jesus.

It is Jesus who works with us to confirm the word.

HEALING REVISION

1. What does Jehovah Rapha mean?

   ....

   ....

2. According to Psalm 103:2-3, healing is one of the benefits of being a Christian.   *True or False*

3. Jesus suffered in every area of life in order to set us free, so we don't have to suffer.   *True or False*

4. Write out and memorise Isaiah 53:4,5 & 6.

   ....

   ....

   ....

5. The words 'griefs' and 'sorrows' in Isaiah 53:4 could equally be translated .... and ....

6. Write out and memorise 1 Peter 2:24.

   ....

   ....

7. Who is the author of sickness and disease?

   ....

8. Write out one scripture that proves God wants us well.

   ....

   ....

9. What is the scripture that proves we are redeemed from the curse of the law?

   ....

   ....

10. If Jesus healed the sick when He was on the earth, write out a scripture that proves he will still heal the sick today.

    ....

    ....

    ....

Chapter Thirteen

NINE STEPS TO DIVINE HEALING

1. Remember, sickness is from Satan.

Be settled in your own heart and mind that sickness is not from God - it originates from Satan.

2. Know it is God's will to heal you.

Be settled in your own heart and mind that it is the will of God to heal you. Jesus came to do the will of God (John 6:38) and never once did He refuse healing to those who came in faith. Do not pray "*....if it be Thy will.*" To doubt God's will is to doubt God's promises. What God has promised, He is willing and able to do. Moreover, as sickness is the "oppression of the devil", it is obviously God's will to set you free. (Acts 10:38)

3. Cast aside all fear!

Jesus said, *"Fear not; believe only and (you) shall be made whole."* (Luke 8:50) The Bible frequently exhorts us to fear not. Fear undermines our faith. Kenneth Copeland says, *"Fear tolerated is faith contaminated."* We must deal with our fears first, then exercise our faith in the promises of God.

4. Forgive everybody.

Mark 11:25-26 shows that unforgiveness is very definitely a hindrance to receiving answers to our prayers - *"And when ye stand praying, forgive, if ye have ought against any; that your Father also which is in heaven may forgive you your trespasses. But if ye do not forgive, neither will your Father which is in heaven forgive your trespasses."* Take the initiative and sincerely forgive all who have sinned against you or have done you wrong or harm. Don't hold a grudge or have bitterness towards another person. Allow God's love to remove it from your life. Now allow God's forgiveness and love to flow through you to all others.

5. Have a positive attitude of mind!

Where there is true faith in a person's heart, it is shown in a positive, cheerful and confident attitude. Learn to think, speak and act positively. There is tremendous power in positive believing. Jesus said, *"If thou canst believe, all things are possible to him that believeth"* Mark 9:23.

6. Base your faith on God's promises.

Read many times over and over the scriptures given in these notes and any others that are of special meaning to you. Learn to base your faith, not on your feelings nor your circumstances, but on the infallible promise of God and His Word.

7. Release your faith, in the Name of Jesus

We all have a measure of faith (Romans 12:3). The only difference is that some use their faith and others don't. Faith must be released to be effective. Sooner or later, there comes a time when your faith is turned loose - perhaps as you read this teaching, or when hands are laid on you in the Name of Jesus, or some other time when you definitely release your faith and put it into action.

> Acts 3:16 states, *"And his name through faith in his name has made this man strong, whom you see and know: yes, the faith which is by him has given him this perfect soundness in the presence of you all."*

Notice it was the **Name of Jesus** and faith in that name that got the man healed.

8. Resist the symptoms.

Recognise that sickness originated from the devil, and God is the author of your healing. Learn to resist the devil, and as the Bible says, *"he will flee from you."* James 4:7. We do not deny the symptoms for they are real enough, but we deny their right and power to remain any longer in our bodies in the face of God's mighty promises on which we now believe, and base our faith, standing steadfast, knowing that, *"what God has promised, He is also willing and able to perform."* (Romans 4:21).

Now do something you could not do! Remember, **faith is an act.** (James 1:22).

9. Praise and thank God continually.

Praise is joyously thanking God for something He has done or promised to do. So then in regard to your healing, thank God continually by saying that *"by the stripes that Jesus bore for me at the Cross of Calvary, I was healed."* (Taken from 1 Peter 2:24).

In 1 Corinthians 15:57, it says that *"praise or thanks to God gives you victory through our Lord Jesus Christ."*

Remember, *"Death and life are in the power of the tongue"* (Proverbs 18:21). So watch the words of your mouth. Only say what God says about your healing and future and trust in Him to bring it to pass. Thank Him, that in the mighty **Name of Jesus**, you are healed!

NINE STEPS TO DIVINE HEALING REVISION

Your homework for this lesson is to go over and over these nine points, and study the scriptures and footnote below.

The following are some scriptures from God's word for you to meditate on and use to build your faith for healing. Remember, Romans 10:17, *"So then faith cometh by hearing, and hearing by the word of God."*

"And ye shall know the truth, and the truth shall make you free." John 8:32.

"Jesus Christ the same yesterday, and today, and forever" Hebrews 13:8.

"Every good gift and every perfect gift is from above, and cometh down from the Father of lights, with whom is no variableness, neither shadow of turning." James 1:17.

"Surely he hath borne our griefs, and carried our sorrows: yet we did esteem him stricken, smitten of God, and afflicted. But he was wounded for our transgressions, he was bruised for our iniquities: the chastisement of our peace was upon him; and with his stripes we are healed." Isaiah 53:4-5.

"And ye shall serve the LORD your God, and he shall bless thy bread, and thy water; and I will take sickness away from the midst of thee." Exodus 23:25.

"And said, If thou wilt diligently hearken to the voice of the LORD thy God, and wilt do that which is right in his sight..... for I am the LORD that healeth thee." Exodus 15:26. [1]

Boldly declare, in the Name of Jesus that God is your Healer!

"Beloved, I wish above all things that thou mayest prosper and be in health, even as thy soul prospereth." 3 John 1:2.

Joyously thank and praise Him, that you are healed and prospering in your day!

(For further teaching, please obtain Pastor's Shaun's book on '101 Divine Healing Facts'.)

Footnote: [1] In the Old Testament, God revealed Himself to His people by His redemptive names, here we see *'I am the Lord that heals you'* is Jehovah Rapha. The word Jehovah in Hebrew means that God is the self-existent One who is forever, always bringing Himself into existence. He is the Life-Giver, Creator, He who brings things to pass, the performer of His Promises. Rapha in the Hebrew means to heal. To be completely healed, become fresh. Rapha also means, physician. It means to take care of and to be repaired or healed. So we could say that God is the Healer.

God who is always bringing His promises to pass in our lives, because it is His divine will, promise and purpose that you be healed, repaired, renewed and made whole. Remember, Jesus came to earth to do the will of His Father. He went to the cross and paid the price for your healing, as well as your sins. God wants you well. His desire is for you to enjoy your life and all of the blessings He has provided for us in Jesus.

CHAPTER FOURTEEN

LAYING ON OF HANDS

    ∾   ∿

> "They shall lay hands on the sick, and they shall recover." (Mark 16:18).

Here in the Book of Mark 16:15-18, we read the last minute instruction of Jesus Christ to His followers before He was taken up into heaven to sit on the right hand of God.

His last eleven words were - *"they (believers) shall lay hands on the sick, they shall recover,"* that means to get well, be healed, not be sick anymore.

God Releases His Power Through Laying on of Hands

I will be explaining in this teaching that laying on of hands is a doctrine of the Church, a doctrine of Christ.

Today, in many churches, we are not laying hands on anyone. Many of our churches are not practising or carrying out this doctrine. Many churches are not obeying Jesus Christ and

His commands in this area. As you would have already noticed from the above scripture, we are commanded by Jesus to lay hands on the sick in faith to release the healing power of God into people's bodies to see them get well and recover.

> *"If you are willing and obedient, you will eat the good of the land"* (Isaiah 1:19).

If we want to experience the power of God in our lives, if we want to see God at work in our churches, if we want His blessings to flow in our midst, then we must be prepared to obey Him. We must be prepared to carry out His words and be doers of His Word.

> ***"BUT BE YE DOERS OF THE WORD, AND NOT HEARERS ONLY, DECEIVING YOUR OWN SELVES"*** (James 1:22).

Regardless of the Christian church we may go to, Jesus Christ is our Lord, and to be followers of Him, we must obey Him by doing what He says in His Word.

You see, by faith in the name of Jesus, as you lay hands on someone's sick body, God's powers will flow through your hands and into that sick body, and the miracle healing powers of God will begin to work there, and that sick body will recover or get well.

Jesus said if you love Him, you were to keep His commandments (John 14:23). You must obey Jesus, not men, or man's traditions and ideas, but rather you must obey the Word of God.

The laying on of hands is a Doctrine of the Church.

The Bible says in Romans 1:16 that the gospel of Christ is the power of God unto salvation.

> *"For I am not ashamed of the gospel of Christ: for it is the power of God unto salvation to every one that believeth; to the Jew first, and also to the Greek. For therein is the righteousness of God revealed from faith to faith: as it is written, The just shall live by faith"* (Romans 1:16,17).

The Gospel of Christ or doctrines of Christ are for us today, because, *"Jesus is the same yesterday, today, and forever"* Hebrews 13:8.

They are the power of God unto salvation, and all the blessings of God for today. Laying on of hands is one of those doctrines of Christ.

The blessings of God will not come from heaven through the doctrines of men. They are only through the doctrines of Christ, revealed to our hearts by the Spirit of God.

> *"This people draweth nigh unto Me with their mouth, and honoureth Me with their lips; but their heart is far from Me. But in vain they do worship me, teaching for doctrines the commandments of men"* (Matthew 15:8 & 9).

Notice here in the book of Matthew that God is speaking, telling and warning you that many people on earth say with their mouth that they worship Him, and honour Him - but God says it is in vain, because they are teaching for doctrines the commandments of men. You are not supposed to obey any commandments or doctrines of man.

> Remember, *"Thus have ye made the commandment of God to no effect by your tradition"* (Matthew 15:6b).

Every doctrine that is not scriptural is a doctrine of man.

If any man tells you, (or for that matter, any pastor or religious leader), that laying on of hands is not important, or it is not for today, I don't care who he is or how many letters he may have behind his name, he is wrong and his doctrine is of man and not of God. The blessings of God to heal the sick will not come through someone like that, who does not believe in the words of Jesus.

I have ministered the word in many countries of the earth including, the Philippines, in Australia, in Czechoslovakia, India, Canada, South Africa, Sierra Leone, Malawi, Zambia, Zimbabwe, USA, Solomon Islands, Kenya, Ethiopia, Vanuatu, Papua New Guinea, Fiji, Samoa etc. After people have heard and believed the Word of God, I have personally laid hands on thousands of people, and in the name of Jesus, seen many hundreds healed as God's power flowed out through my hands and into their bodies.

Not all these healings were instantaneous, although many were, yet many from that point of contact began to recover and get well. I have seen legs grow longer and people throw down their walking sticks, as God's power flowed through their bodies and healed them. Remember, *"Jesus is the same yesterday, today and forever"* Hebrews 13:8.

"Therefore, leaving the principles of the doctrine of Christ, let us go unto perfection; not laying again the foundations of repentance from dead works, and of faith toward God, of the doctrine of baptisms, and of laying on of hands, and of resurrection of the dead, and of eternal judgment" (Hebrews 6:1&2).

Here we see in the Book of Hebrews, that the doctrine of laying on of hands that Jesus taught, is listed as a foundation principle that all believers should know before they can go on to maturity (perfection) in the body of Christ.

Many churches believe in baptism, but leave out the doctrine of laying on of hands, yet we can see here the two go hand in hand. The minds of men in these last days have deleted many of the doctrines of Christ from their church services and because of this, they are not seeing the power of God in manifestation.

Any doctrine that cannot be substantiated by scripture and verse is wrong and is from the minds of men.

All doctrine must be backed up by the word of God taken in context with the chapter from where it came.

<u>Let me bring a warning from the Bible:</u>

"Now the Spirit speaketh expressly, that in the latter times some shall depart from the faith, giving heed to seducing spirits, and doctrines of devils" (1 Timothy 4:1).

The devil tells man's mind that it is okay to take things out of the Bible and say they are not for today. But it isn't. It is wrong to delete doctrines that will set men free; it is wrong not to preach and teach the truth, because the truth in God's Word when revealed, sets men free.

The devil wants you to be sick and die, but God wants you to be well and prosper even as your soul prospers (3 John 2). God tells us in Exodus 15:26, *"I am the Lord that healeth thee."* He will release His mighty power to work in and through us as we obey Him and lay our hands on people to see them healed.

"Till I come, give attendance to reading, to exhortation, to doctrine. Neglect not the gift that is in thee, which was given thee by prophecy, with the laying on of the hands of the presbytery" (1 Timothy 4:13 &14).

Here Paul told Timothy to give attention to doctrine, and not to neglect the gift that was given him by the laying on of hands.

The power of God will flow through anyone's hands if they are a believer and take God at His Word, and in faith, lay their hands on the sick in the name of Jesus.

You are a candidate for the power of God to flow through your hands to heal the sick. You can begin in faith by praying for your own family and friends and laying hands on them (with their permission, of course) to see them recover and get well.

> *"Till I come, give attendance to reading, to exhortation, to doctrine. Neglect not the gift that is in thee, which was given thee by prophecy, with the laying on of the hands of the presbytery. Meditate upon these things; give thyself wholly to them; that thy profiting may appear to all. Take heed unto thyself, and unto the doctrine; continue in them: for in doing this thou shalt both save thyself, and them that hear thee"* (1 Timothy 4:13-16).

Isn't that beautiful? God has given us such a simple doctrine. It doesn't cost anything. We just lift our hands and lay them on some individual who needs help, and God does the rest. That is what God has done for believers who believe in Him.

People have to be trained and taught to believe in the Bible.

> *"The Father loveth the Son, and hath given all things into His hand"* John 3:35.

Into His what? Into His Hand!

Let us read Matthew 28:18-20.

> *"And Jesus came and spake unto them, saying, 'All power is given unto Me in heaven and in the earth.'*

> *Go ye therefore, and teach all nations, baptizing them in the name of the Father, and of the Son, and of the Holy Ghost: Teaching them to observe all things whatsoever I have commanded you: and lo, I am with you always, even unto the end of the world. Amen."*

Jesus has all power and all authority, and He has now told us to go in His name in that power and authority and make disciples teaching them to observe all the things that He has commanded us to do, and He will be with us. Well, one of those things is to heal the sick!

> Let us read Matthew 10:1, *"And when He had called unto Him His twelve disciples, He gave them power against unclean spirits, to cast them out, and to heal all manner of sickness and all manner of disease."*

> And Acts 5:12 says, *"And by the hands of the apostles were many signs and wonders wrought among the people; (and they were all with one accord in Solomon's porch).* See? Hands of the apostles!

Now remember once again, Mark 16:18, These signs will follow the believers, *"They will lay hands on the sick and they shall recover."* If we obey Him, His mighty power flows through us. If we don't, His people suffer, and it is not His fault.

The doctrine of Laying on of Hands as found in the Word is for more than just healing.

We will now cover, fifteen other ways in which we can scripturally use our hands as an instrument through which God's supernatural power can flow to bring blessings, as found in the Word of God.

1. To Bless the Family

> *"And Joseph took them both, Ephraim in his right hand toward Israel's left hand, and Manasseh in his left hand toward Israel's right hand, and brought them near unto him. And Israel stretched out his right hand, and laid it upon Ephraim's head, who was the younger, and his left hand upon Manasseh's head, guiding his hands wittingly; for Manasseh was the firstborn.*
>
> *And he blessed Joseph, and said, 'God, before whom my father Abraham and Isaac did walk, the God which fed me all my life long unto this day. The Angel which redeemed me from all evil, bless the lads; and let my name be named on them, and the name of my fathers Abraham and Isaac; and let them grow into a multitude in the midst of the earth"* (Genesis 48:13-16).

Here we see Israel (Jacob) by faith imparting a blessing to his grandchildren, and by faith prophesying a good future, as he lays his hands upon their heads.

2. To Transfer Blessings

> "And Joshua the son of Nun was full of the spirit of wisdom; for Moses had laid his hands upon him: and the children of Israel hearkened unto him, and did as the Lord commanded Moses" (Deuteronomy 34:9).

Moses had imparted to Joshua a spirit of wisdom by laying his hands upon him. Now the anointing on Moses' life was upon Joshua to lead and guide this great nation of Israel.

3. Imparting 'The Blessing'

> "Then were there brought unto Him little children, that He should put His hands on them, and pray: and the disciples rebuked them. But Jesus said, 'Suffer the little children, and forbid them not come unto me: for of such is the kingdom of heaven.' And he laid hands on them and departed thence" (Matthew 19:13-15).

Here, because of His great love for children, Jesus imparted 'The Blessing'. He demonstrated this by the laying on of hands and speaking words of faith. Here we see how important it is to God to impart 'The Blessing' to all that come to Him. We also get to see this practical demonstration through the life and ministry of Jesus.

4. **To Heal**

"*Now when the sun was setting, all they that had any sick with different diseases brought them unto Him; and He laid His hands on every one of them, and healed them*" (Luke 4:40).

"*And Ananias went his way, and entered into the house; and putting his hands on him and said, 'Brother Saul, the Lord, even Jesus, that appeared unto thee in the way as thou camest, hath sent me, that you might receive your sight, and be filled with the Holy Ghost*" (Acts 9:17).

5. **To Ordain**

"*Whom they set before the apostles: and when they had prayed, they laid their hands on them*" (Acts 6:6).

"*And thou shalt bring the Levites before the Lord: and the children of Israel shall put their hands upon the Levites: And Aaron shall offer the Levites before the Lord for an offering of the children of Israel, that they may execute the service of the Lord*" (Numbers 8:10,11).

6. **To Send Out Missionaries**

   "As they ministered to the Lord, and fasted, the Holy Ghost said, Separate Me Barnabas and Saul for the work whereunto I have called them. And when they had fasted and prayed, and laid their hands on them, they sent them away" (Acts 13:2,3).

7. **To Baptise in the Spirit**

   "Then laid they their hands on them, and they received the Holy Ghost. And then Simon saw that through laying on of the apostles' hands the Holy Ghost was given" (Acts 8:17,18).

   "And when Paul had laid his hands upon them, the Holy Ghost came on them; and they spoke with tongues, and prophesied" (Acts 19:6).

8. **To Work Miracles**

   "Therefore they stayed there a long time, speaking boldly in the Lord, who was bearing witness to the word of His grace, granting signs and wonders to be done by their hands" (Acts 14:3 NKJV).

   "And God wrought special miracles by the hands of Paul" (Acts 19:11).

9. **To Fellowship**

"And when James, Cephas, and John, who seemed to be pillars, perceived the grace that was given unto me, they gave to me and Barnabas the right hands of fellowship; that we should go unto the heathen, and they unto the Jews" (Galatians 2:9).

10. **To Impart Gifts**

"Neglect not the gift that is in thee, which was given thee by prophecy with the laying on of the hands of the presbytery" (1 Timothy 4:14).

11. **To Use Wisdom**

"Lay hands suddenly on no man, neither be partaker of other men's sins: keep thyself pure" (1 Timothy 5:22).

In all of the ways in which we use our hands for God's power to flow through, we must use wisdom. Whether it be to ordain, send forth people or healing, etc. Let's not do it suddenly - let's make sure first, we are in faith, and in God's will and that what we are doing is not in any way going to cause an offence. It is no good laying hands on people if they don't want hands laid on them.

"And Joshua the son of Nun was full of the spirit of wisdom; for Moses had laid his hands upon him: and

the children of Israel hearkened unto him, and did as the Lord commanded Moses" (Deuteronomy 34:9).

So let's heed this warning - all things must be done to edify and bring blessing.

12. To Stir up Gifts

"Wherefore I put thee in remembrance that thou stir up the gift of God, which is in thee by the putting on of my hands. For God has not given us the spirit of fear; but of power, and of love, and of a sound mind" (2 Timothy 1:6&7).

Outcomes and Results

Let us now look at some of the many great miracles and healings that have been given by God as His power has been released through believers' hands.

Mark 6:2-6, *"And when the Sabbath day was come, He began to teach in the synagogue: and many hearing Him were astonished, saying, 'From whence hath this man these things? And what wisdom is this, which is given unto Him, that even such mighty works are wrought by His hands?*

Is not this the carpenter, and son of Mary, the brother of James, and Joseph, and of Judah, and Simon? and are not His sisters here with us?' And they were offended at Him. But Jesus said unto them, 'A prophet is not without honour, but in his own country, and among his own kin, and in his own house.' And He could there do no mighty work, save that He laid His hands upon a few sick folk, and healed them. And He marvelled because of their unbelief. And He went round about the villages teaching."

Mark 7:32,35: "And they bring unto Him one that was deaf, and had an impediment in his speech; and they beseech Him to put His hand upon him. And straightaway his ears were opened, and the string of his tongue was loosed, and he spoke plain."

Mark 8:22-25: "And He cometh to Bethsaida; and they bring a blind man unto Him, and besought Him to touch him. And He took the blind man by the hand, and led him out of the town; and when he had spat on his eyes, and put His hands upon him, He asked him if he saw anything. And he looked up, and said, 'I see men as trees, walking.' After that, He put His hands again upon his eyes, and made him look: and he was restored, and saw every man clearly."

Remember, God watches over His Word to perform it. (Jeremiah 1:12).

Mark 1:40-42: *"And there came a leper to Him, beseeching Him, and kneeling down to Him, and saying unto Him, 'If Thou wilt, Thou canst make me clean.' And Jesus, moved with compassion, put forth His hand and touched him, and saith unto him, 'I will; be thou clean.' And as soon as He had spoken, immediately the leprosy departed from him, and he was cleansed."*

Luke 4:40: *"Now when the sun was setting, all they that had any sick with different diseases brought they unto Him; and He laid His hands on every one of them and healed them."*

Luke 13:13: *"And He laid His hands on her: and immediately she was made straight, and glorified God."*

Matthew 8:15: *"And He touched her hand, and the fever left her: and she arose, and ministered unto them."*

Matthew 9:18: *"While He spake these things unto them, behold, there came a certain ruler, and worshiped Him, saying, 'My daughter is even now dead: but come and lay Thy hand upon her, and she shall live."*

It works for Paul and Peter and others as well.

Acts 28:8: *"And it came to pass, that the father of Publius lay sick of a fever and of a bloody flux: to whom Paul entered in, and prayed, and laid his hands on him, and healed him."*

Acts 8:14-17: *"Now when the apostles which were at Jerusalem heard that Samaria had received the Word of God, they sent unto them Peter and John: Who, when they were come down, prayed for them, that they might receive the Holy Ghost: (for as yet He was fallen upon none of them: only they were baptized in the name of the Lord Jesus Christ). Then laid their hands on them, and they received the Holy Ghost."*

Acts 19:11: *"And God wrought special miracles by the hands of Paul."*

It has worked for hundreds of times for me, Shaun Marler, and it will also work for you, if you will trust and obey.

The power of God will flow through your hands. You will experience miracles and healings and see people get well.

Let Jesus train you in the doctrine of laying on of hands. Be led by the Spirit of God. Seek wisdom and righteousness, and you will be satisfied.

2 Timothy 2:15 says, *"Study to shew thyself approved unto God, a workman that needeth not to be ashamed, rightly dividing the Word of truth."*

LAYING ON OF HANDS REVISION

1. Jesus taught believers to lay hands on the sick. Write out scriptural reference and memorize.
   ....
   ....

2. The laying on of hands is a doctrine of the church.
   True or False

3. Write out and memorize James 1:22.
   ....
   ....

4. According to Matthew 15:6, what has made the commandments (Word) of God to no effect?
   ....
   ....

5. Which scripture in the bible lists laying on of hands as a doctrine of Christ? Write out and memorize.
   ....
   ....
   ....

6. It is wrong to delete doctrines of Christ from the Word of God?   *True or False*

7. In 1 Timothy 4:13 & 14, we are commanded to give attention to doctrine. This means that we should lay hands on the sick according to the Word of God.
True or False

8. List some of the blessings that can be imparted through the laying on of hands. Give scriptural references.
....
....
....
....

9. Write out and memorize a powerful scripture where the laying on of hands was used for healing the sick.
....
....
....

Chapter Fifteen

GIVING AND RECEIVING

Solomon was known not only for his **wisdom** but also for his enormous **wealth**!

Solomon **remembered** the Lord, *"for it is the Lord who gave him the ability to produce wealth, that he may establish His covenant which He swore unto his fathers, as it is this day."* Deuteronomy 8:18.

In Proverbs 3:9 Solomon wrote, *"Honour the Lord with your wealth, and with the first-fruits of all your crops, then your barns will be filled to overflowing, and your vats will brim over with new wine."*

Solomon was the **wisest** and **wealthiest** man who ever lived. If we had a success seminar today and he was the guest speaker, he would be top of his field, best in the world, a man to sit up and take notice of. What this man had to say obviously worked - he was living walking proof and he had the results (wealth) to back up what he said to be true.

He had credibility and notoriety and the respect of his peers of his day. And he said 'if you people want the key to be a success, if you want to prosper beyond your **wildest dreams**, then here is the answer.'

> Proverbs 3:1 10: *"My son, forget not my law; but let thine heart keep my commandments: for length of days, and long life, and peace, shall they add to thee. Let not mercy and truth forsake thee; bind them about thy neck; write them upon the tablet of thine heart: So shalt thou find favour and good understanding in the sight of God and man. Trust in the Lord with all thine heart; and lean not unto thine own understanding. In all thy ways acknowledge Him, and He shall direct thy paths. Be not wise in thine own eyes; fear the Lord, and depart from evil. It shall be health to thy navel, and marrow to thy bones. Honour the Lord with thy substance, and with the first-fruits of all thine increase: So shall thy barns be filled with plenty, and thy presses shall burst out with new wine."*

Don't forget God's laws. Let your heart keep His Words (commandments). Trust in God, and honour Him with your substance and your first fruits, and you will have a long, prosperous and healthy life and enjoy abundance.

Because we now live in a Covenant of Grace, then our lasting prosperity (with peace) is come by our knowledge of God and of Jesus our Lord.

"Grace and peace be multiplied unto you through the knowledge of God, and of Jesus our Lord." (2 Peter 1:2)

Paul Calls Giving a Grace

Romans 12:6 & 8 - *"Having then gifts differing according to the grace that is given to us, whether prophecy, let us prophesy according to the proportion of faith;*

Or he that exhorteth, on exhortation: he that giveth, let him do it with simplicity; he that ruleth, with diligence; he that sheweth mercy, with cheerfulness."

Malachi 3:10 - *"Bring ye all the tithes into the storehouse, that there may be meat in mine house, and prove me now herewith, saith the Lord of hosts, if I will not open you the windows of heaven, and pour you out a blessing, that there shall not be room enough to receive it."*

Malachi 3:11 - *" And I will rebuke the devourer for your sakes, and he shall not destroy the fruits of your ground; neither shall your vine cast her fruit before the time in the field, saith the Lord of hosts."*

We can put God to the test by putting Proverbs 3:9 into action and Malachi 3:10 by giving *in faith* with a joyous heart, and knowing God will multiply our seed sown. God has given us the power (and wisdom) to get wealth. He wants us to give and prove Him, put Him to the test and see Him fill up our barns and our vats (storehouses, bank accounts), because God wants to establish His covenant that He swore to Abraham. He promised to make Abraham and his seed rich. (If you are Christ's, then are you Abraham's seed and heirs according to the promise. Galatians 3:29.)

But before God can do it, we have to fulfil our part. In order for God to establish His covenant, we must obey His Word, and sow seeds of finance, so God can cause them to become a bumper crop.

Grace enables us to see our tithe as a gift from God being richly sown into God's Kingdom for His ultimate purposes. Everything good we have is a gift from God.

> 2 Corinthians 9:6 12 - *" But this I say, He which soweth sparingly shall reap also sparingly; and he which soweth bountifully shall reap also bountifully. Every man according as he purposeth in his heart, so let him give; not grudgingly, or of necessity: for God loveth a cheerful giver. And God is able to make all grace abound toward you; that ye always having all sufficiency in all things, may abound to every good work: (as it is written, 'He hath dispersed abroad; he hath given to the poor: His righteousness remaineth forever. Now he that ministereth seed to the sower both minister bread for your food, and multiply your*

seed sown, and increase the fruits of your righteousness;) being enriched in every thing to all bountifulness, which causeth through us thanksgiving to God. For the administration of this service not only supplieth the want of the saints, but is abundant also by many thanksgivings unto God."

Many Christians want to reap a financial harvest, without first planting any seed!

Ask any farmer, it does not work that way. If you want to reap a harvest, you must first plant your field.

Also, the harvest that you will eventually reap after the seeds have been planted and allowed time to grow, and plants come to maturity and fruits be ready for the picking, will be in direct relation to the size of crop you first planted in the ground.

If you plant a small crop, you will reap a small harvest.

If you plant a large crop, you will reap a large harvest.

Which brings me to another point.

I would like to say right here - Don't despise small beginnings!

Remember the widow's mite?

> Mark 12:42 44 - "And there came a certain poor widow, and she threw in two mites, which make a

farthing. And He called unto Him His disciples, and saith unto them, 'Verily I say unto you, That this poor widow hath cast more in, than all they which have cast into the treasury: for all they did cast in of their abundance; but she of her want did cast in all that she had, even all her living'."

She had only sowed a small amount in comparison to what others were sowing, but in actual fact, she had sown the largest crop, and would ultimately reap the largest harvest, because she had sown all that she had. The others had sown out of their abundance, so in comparison, their giving was no real sacrifice to them, but this little widow lady had sown all that she had. This was a great sacrifice; this was abundance (even though the gift was small).

By sowing in love into the work of God (even though she could not really afford it) this little lady had now put herself in line for a mighty blessing, a mighty harvest.

You may ask; Shaun, how do you know this?

Well, we can see here that her offering caught the eyes of God. Jesus Himself commented on this lady's faith in giving. It's been recorded eternally in God's Word.

You see, what you do in faith and love does not go unnoticed by our God.

Remember the scripture we read in 2 Corinthians 9:10 - *"Now He that ministereth seed to the sower both minister bread for your food, and multiply your seed sown, and increase the fruits of your righteousness."*

God is able to multiply your seed sown and increase your fruits or the return of that crop. Even though the gift was small, it was in actual fact large, because she was sowing in famine, sowing all she had. By doing this, she was putting a spiritual law into motion! God would now multiply her seed sown, so she could reap back an increased harvest.

> Remember Philippians 4:19 - *"But my God shall supply all your need according to His riches in glory by Christ Jesus."*

Let's look at Genesis 26: Verse 1 - *"And there was a famine in the land ...., (verse 12) then Isaac sowed in that land, and received in the same year a hundredfold; and the Lord blessed him."*

Here Isaac sowed in famine, and in the same year reaped a hundredfold. Let's say that again:

He sowed in famine, and in the same year reaped a hundredfold!

This widow lady had sown in famine, and now could expect a hundredfold in that same year.

Let's look at another widow lady in God's Word with a similar experience -

1 Kings 17:8 16, *"And the word of the Lord came unto*

him (Elijah), saying, 'Arise, get thee to Zarephath, which belongeth to Zidon, and dwell there: behold, I have commanded a widow woman there to sustain thee'.

So he arose and went to Zarapheth. And when he came to the gate of the city, behold, the widow woman was there gathering of sticks: and he called to her, and said, 'Fetch me, I pray thee, a little water in a vessel, that I may drink.' And as she was going to fetch it, he called to her and said, 'Bring me, I pray thee, a morsel of bread in thine hand.'

And she said, 'As the Lord thy God liveth, I have not a cake, but a handful of meal in a barrel, and a little oil in a cruse: and, behold, I am gathering two sticks, that I may go in and dress it for me and my son, that we may eat and die.'

And Elijah said unto her, 'Fear not: go and do as thou hast said: but make me thereof a little cake first, and bring it unto me, and after make for thee and for thy son. For thus saith the Lord God of Israel, - The barrel of meal shall not waste, neither shall the cruse of oil fail, until the day that the Lord sendeth rain upon the earth.'

And she went and did according to the saying of Elijah: and she, and he, and her house, did eat many days. And the barrel of meal wasted not, neither did the cruse of oil fail, according to the Word of the Lord, which He spake by Elijah."

Here this lady sowed in famine - she sowed her last meal into the Kingdom of God. She sowed into the work of the ministry by feeding the prophet of God. Notice she fed him *first*? She took care of God's work first! A lot of Christians want to take care of their own affairs first, their own family first, and give to God out of what is left over; but this does not open the windows of heaven.

What opens the windows of heaven is putting God in first place: giving God your first fruits of all your increase, paying your tithes upfront. (Now that brings me to a point that we will cover later and that is whether or not under this covenant, we have to pay tithes).

You see, this widow lady put the work of God first, and by so doing you saw what happened, she sowed in famine, and reaped a hundredfold. The bowl of meal and cruse of oil did not run dry.

That one meal she sowed in the work of the ministry, (when she herself and her family were in a desperate situation) opened the windows of heaven, and God sustained her all those years, while famine was in the land. Neither she, her son, nor the prophet went hungry.

Now I would like to lay a few ground rules and establish some basic spiritual principles and laws:

1. It is God's will for you to prosper.

"Beloved, I wish above all things that thou mayest prosper and be in health, even as thy soul prospereth." 3 John 2.

See, here God wishes that we prosper and be in health, even as our soul prospers.

2. We must give and sow seeds in order to reap.

"And God said, Let the earth bring forth grass, the herb yielding seed and the fruit tree yielding fruit after his kind, whose seed is in itself, upon the earth; and it was so. And the earth brought forth grass, and herb yielding seed after his kind, and the tree yielding fruit, whose seed was in itself, after his kind: and God saw that it was good." Genesis 1:11,12.

"While the earth remaineth, seedtime and harvest, and cold and heat, and summer and winter, and day and night shall not cease." Genesis 8:22

"Be not deceived; God is not mocked: for whatsoever a man soweth, that shall he also reap." Galatians 6:7.

> "Bring ye all the tithes into the storehouse, that there may be meat in mine house, and prove me now herewith, saith the Lord of hosts, if I will not open you the windows of heaven, and pour you out a blessing, that there shall not be room enough to receive it." Malachi 3:10.

3. Tithes and offerings are a way of honouring God.

> "Honour the Lord with thy substance, and with the first fruits of all thine increase; so shall thy barns be filled with plenty, and thy presses shall burst out with new wine." Proverbs 3:9,10.

In the ancient world, people of all religions would pay ten percent of their wealth to the object of their worship, as a means of worship and honour.

4. Don't Rob God.

> In Malachi 3:8 it says: "Will a man rob God? Yet ye have robbed Me. But ye say, 'Wherein have we robbed Thee?' In tithes and offerings."

God's Word here tells us that ten percent of all we have and earn actually belongs to God and it is to be used for the purpose of spreading the Gospel.

Now you might say: *"Well, all we have belongs to God"*, and that is true, but from this scripture, we can see that God specifically lays claim to ten percent of all your earnings for the express purpose of spreading the Gospel.

After that, you sow your offerings according to your faith. But let's not forget all the teaching. God is not robbing us! He wants us to give in order for the Kingdom to expand, but in the same scripture, Malachi 3:10 promises an abundant return on all your giving.

So don't give grudgingly, give cheerfully, knowing that, 1. you are helping to spread the Gospel, and 2. you are investing in a mighty work and are promised an abundant return.

5. Once you have sown, be patient, and wait for the return.

> Ecclesiastes 11:1 - *"Cast your bread upon the waters: for thou shalt find it after many days."*

> Mark 4: 8 and 20: *"And other (seed) fell on good ground and did yield fruit that sprang up and increased: and brought forth, some thirty, and some sixty, and some a hundred. And these are they which are sown on good ground; such as hear the word, and receive it, and bring forth fruit, some thirty-fold, some sixty, and some a hundred."*

Genesis 8:22 - *"While the earth remaineth, seedtime and harvest, and cold and heat, and summer and winter, and day and night shall not cease."*

Hebrews 6:12 - *"That ye be not slothful, but followers of them who through faith and patience inherit the promises."*

Remember, there is a time period between when you sow and when you reap. Give time for crops to grow.

6. Don't stop giving.

Ecclesiastes 11:4 - *"He that observeth the wind shall not sow; and he that regardeth the clouds shall not reap."*

Don't be stopped in giving because conditions aren't favourable. If you do, you won't reap. E.g. If you say, 'Well, I've got insurance due next month, car registration or other circumstances arising, I'd better stop my giving', then the devil will always make sure you have plenty of bills, so you will never give, never plant and never reap.

Yes, you must be wise and responsible and pay your dues, but plan your finances and don't eat all your "seed". Don't spend your last dollar, give it away. Plant some seed in the gospel to ensure a harvest. Like we have already pointed out, plant seed in the Kingdom first, give God your best, your first-fruits, and God will give you His best.

7. Let Your Seed Die.

Some people want to give their tithes and offerings and then try to tell the pastor of the church what to do with it, like it's still their money. People like to control and use their giving as leverage, but this is totally wrong.

Once you have given something, it is no longer yours. If you are giving, but not yet truly releasing it, it will not do you any good.

> The Bible says: *"Verily, verily, I say unto you, Except a corn of wheat fall into the ground and die, it abideth alone: but if it die, it bringeth forth much fruit."* John 12:24.

That seed must fall into the ground and die first if it is going to produce and bring forth a harvest. When a farmer plants his seed in the dirt, that seed then, as far as he is concerned is rendered useless. He can't sell it, he can't eat it, he can't even use it to feed his animals.

But this is where the seed dies, and the law of sowing and reaping takes over, and this seed will now die and bring forth life and reproduce itself, some thirty, sixty and one hundred-fold.

So likewise, we must render our finances useless. Once we have given and sown them, as far as we are concerned, they are dead and gone. Then let faith in God and His Word take control and God will multiply your seed sown and increase the fruits of your righteousness and supply all your needs.

David said that he wouldn't sacrifice to God anything that didn't cost him something.

> 2 Samuel 24:24 - *"And the king said unto Araunah, Nay; but I will surely buy it of thee at a price: neither will I offer burnt offerings unto the Lord my God of that which doth cost me nothing. So David bought the threshing floor and the oxen for fifty shekels of silver."*

David paid a price - he rendered his seed dead in order to bring a gift to God. Remember, the tithe is God's not ours. Don't call something that belongs to God, yours.

> Luke 17:1 says, *"Then said He unto the disciples, It is impossible but that offences will come: but woe unto him, through whom they come!"*

In context here, Jesus said if offences are going to come, and they definitely will, they will come over money - for this teaching here in Luke 16 and 17 is all about stewardship - and people seem easily to get offended over the topic of money.

> In Malachi 3:7 12, it says: *"Even from the days of your fathers ye are gone away from Mine ordinances, and have not kept them. Return unto Me, and I will return unto you, saith the Lord of hosts. But ye said, Wherein shall we return? Will a man rob God?*

> *Yet ye have robbed Me. But ye say, Wherein have we robbed Thee? In tithes and offerings. Ye are cursed with a curse: for ye have robbed Me, even this whole nation. Bring ye all the tithes into the storehouse, that there may be meat in Mine house, and prove Me now herewith, saith the Lord of hosts, if I will not open you the windows of heaven, and pour you out a blessing, that there shall not be room enough to receive it. And I will rebuke the devourer for your sakes, and he shall not destroy the fruits of your ground; neither shall your vine cast her fruit before the time in the field, said the Lord of hosts. And all nations shall call you blessed; for ye shall be a delightsome land, said the Lord of hosts."*

God is saying here that His people have departed from Him in the area of giving. They were robbing Him in the area of tithes and offerings, and this was bringing a curse on them, and even the whole nation. He said if they would repent and return to him and bring the money (meat in) to His house, then something would happen. The windows of heaven would open up and pour forth a constant stream of blessings.

God would then rebuke the devourer, that he would not destroy (a curse would be cut off) and that God's people would be blessed along with the whole land.

8. The Curse Must Be Broken

As I meditated on these scriptures recently, God gave me a revelation concerning this passage, and I would like to share it with you now.

Because the children of Israel had robbed God in the area of finances, there was no meat (substance in His house). This meant that there was no money to pay preachers or priests in order for them to live, so the people who should have been full-time workers were off trying to earn a living instead. Today, many evangelists aren't evangelizing, because there is no money to pay them. Many pastors are working part-time jobs, because there are not enough finances in their church to go full time.

So because of this, God said we are cursed with a curse. Now it's not that God is cursing us, because He isn't. But through sin, there is a curse in the earth. The devil (devourer) uses the strength of sin to push the curse to its fullest, and destroy the people and the land.

God sent Jesus, the Word, to die in our place and redeem us from this curse. The anointing breaks the yoke, the Word declares.

Well, it's like this: even though we have been redeemed through Jesus many people don't realize this, and so the curse is running rampant. But God, through revelation knowledge, sets us free.

> Hosea 4:6, *"My people are destroyed for lack of knowledge."*
>
> John 8:32, *"And ye shall know the truth, and the truth shall make you free."*

But you see, if there is no money in the church because God's people have neglected to put it there;
>
> the pastors are not pastoring;
> the evangelists are not evangelizing;
> the teachers are not teaching, etc. etc.

God is unable to release the revelation knowledge, because the revelation knowledge comes through the fivefold ministry in Ephesians 4:8 12. No anointing in manifestation through the gifts Jesus gave to men, means no revelation knowledge coming forth, and that's what sets us free from the curse - a revelation in our life of the truth of God's Word.

Jesus gave gifts to men, not just the church. A pastor, an evangelist, a teacher, prophet, apostle - they are gifts given to this world to bring God's Word in order to heal and restore people unto God, and bring prosperity and blessing.

Now all Christians have this ministry, but it is the fivefold ministry that equips the laity for the task.

If there is no money in God's house, the work is slowed down through a lack of workers, and the curse is allowed to run loose. Plenty of money means more full-time workers in the field, which means more saints being equipped, which ultimately means more people being saved - more Word being released - more blessing in the land, because people are getting a hold of God.

> *"Bring forth with thee every living thing that is with thee, of all flesh, both of fowl, and of cattle, and of every creeping thing that creepeth upon the earth; that they may breed abundantly in the earth, and be fruitful, and multiply upon the earth."* Genesis 8:17.

God wants to establish His covenant in the earth.

Every promise of God is received by faith, not of works so no person can boast. I remember John Avanzini taught me that debt is not mathematical, it is spiritual. As such, it must be dealt with.

There are many good people that faithfully give and they don't see a return on their giving and this is because the curse of poverty is operating in their lives.

A good friend of mine, Pastor Jim Kibler, shares in his book titled "The Blessing" (it is available through Amazon), that when this revelation came to him, he got completely set free of perpetual debt and now lives in absolute abundance. Pastor Jim also shared with me how that when he was listening to a 'Believers Voice of Victory' program, Kenneth and Gloria Copeland shared how after they broke the curse of poverty and kicked it out of their lives, their finances have never stopped increasing. Pastor Jim also says that, *"A prayer of faith and deliverance must be prayed in order for a person to be set free of debt and lack."*

He says, *"To receive 'The Blessing' flow back into your life, you must deal with the curse of poverty as found in Deuteronomy 28:29."*

"And thou shalt grope at noonday, as the blind gropeth in darkness, and thou shalt not prosper in thy ways: and thou shalt be only oppressed and spoiled evermore, and no man shall save thee."

This is one of the curses mentioned in Deuteronomy 28. Jesus redeemed us from these curses when He died for us on the cross. Just like He paid the price for everyone's healing, but many in the body of Christ, do not believe in healing today and have not appropriated that promise by faith to their life. In the same way, many do not believe or know they are redeemed from the curse of poverty. This blessing must be received and appropriated by faith in our lives.

In order to do this, we must pray a specific prayer to break the curse of poverty off of our lives and finances. Once again in the book of Galatians, the Word of God tells us, "That Christ has redeemed us (bought us back) from the curse of the law." Because He was made and became a curse for us to pay the price for our freedom.

For ye know the grace of our Lord Jesus Christ, that, though he was rich, yet for your sakes, he became poor, that ye through his poverty might be rich. (2 Corinthians 8:9)

Every believer has authority through the name of Jesus to cast out devils. Right now I am going to pray a prayer, so that this devil, curse and spirit of poverty leaves your life, in Jesus Name.

> ***Father, I thank you that right now (add your name) is set free by the blood of Jesus Christ and redeemed from the curse of the law. I command you spirit of poverty and lack to come off my brother/sister, in the mighty name of Jesus I command this and I demand this spirit leave, go from them, their business, their lives and their finances. Father, I now thank you that 'The Blessing of Abraham' comes upon them and finances flow back into their lives, and they prosper abundantly, in the Name of Jesus. Amen!***

"And if ye be Christ's, then are ye Abraham's seed, and heirs according to the promise." (Galatians 3:29)

It is scriptural to bring tithes under this covenant.

In heaven, everyone is going to do things God's way. It would be wise if we would learn that we do not have to wait until we get to heaven to live and act by the principles of God. When it comes to giving, God has a plan for us. It would be wise if we would do it God's way now. God knows how to make us successful. He knows how to let us get the most out of our giving.

Melchizedek - Type of Christ.

"For this Melchizedek, king of Salem, priest of the most high God, who met Abraham returning from the slaughter of the kings, and blessed him; To whom also Abraham gave a tenth part of all; first being by interpretation King of righteousness, and after that also King of Salem, which is King of peace; Without father, without mother, without descent, having neither beginning of days, nor end of life; but made like unto the Son of God; abideth a priest continually. Now consider how great this man was, unto whom even the patriarch Abraham gave the tenth of the spoils. And verily they that are of the sons of Levi, who receive the office of the priesthood, have a commandment to take tithes of the people according to the law, that is, of their brethren, though they come out of the loins of Abraham: But he whose descent is not counted from them received tithes of Abraham, and blessed him that had the promises. And without all contradiction, the less is blessed of the better. And here men that die receive tithes; but there he receiveth them, of whom it is witnessed that he liveth. And as I may so say, Levi also, who receiveth tithes, paid tithes in Abraham. For he was yet in the loins of his father, when Melchisedek met him." Hebrews 7:1-10.

The Eternal Principle

Before the law, *"Abraham gave a tenth part of all"* to Melchizedek (Hebrews 7:2). Long before the Levites were commanded to take a tithe from the people, Abraham gave a tithe to Melchizedek. Before the Mosaic Law was instituted, God instituted tithing into the affairs of man. In fact, many years before the introduction of the law, God led Abraham to give a tithe to Melchizedek. The Levites who later were commanded to take the tithe did not have any choice in the matter; nor did the people. (Hebrews 7:5). They did it because they were commanded to do it.

Our text tells us that tithing was introduced **BEFORE** the law, and it has continued since the law.

"Here men that die receive tithes; but there he receiveth them, of whom it is witness that he liveth."
(Hebrews 7:8)

The author of the epistle to the Hebrews, by the direction of the Holy Spirit, gave us this brief, historical sketch of tithing because the whole purpose of the Bible is to reveal to man the **grace** of God.

On eight occasions in the New Testament, the Apostle Paul calls **giving a grace**. Giving is not a law. Tithing is not a legalistic requirement for us. It is an enlargement of the grace of God in our hearts. **Tithing is the grace of giving**. Never has there been a principle of God that is operating more surely in our day of grace than the principle of tithing.

As concerning the law and the Jew, tithing was merely a starting point. Some of the time they gave a second tithe, sometimes a third, and frequently they also gave freewill offerings. The beautiful tabernacle was constructed out of freewill gifts. Tithing was the starting place.

God simply reminds us here that the principle of tithing is an **eternal principle**. It is one begun before the law, it continued during it, and it still exists today and will continue during the millennium.

The question is asked, *"How is the tithe given to God?"*

The answer is, *"Just as it has always been done: through God's people, through His agents, through His institution."* In our age of Grace, that institution is the Church.

Tithing is an eternal principle. It is a grace gift. If observed carefully, it is God's way of building strong, healthy and happy people for His glory.

Jesus perfected the Mosaic system. He didn't do away with it, He perfected it. How is the tithe perfected?

Can Christ give the tithes for us? No, He cannot. Because He has entrusted us with possessions, and we must give a tithe of what we possess. Can we just give a once and for all offering or tithe? NO! Because we don't get paid all in one go. We must bring in the first fruits of all our increase as we earn it.

We bring out tithes and offerings to God because we love Him and want to honour Him. We want Him to know we are grateful for what He has done. We want there to be money in His house, so He can use it to save and bring others in.

So now, we bring our tithes and offerings not out of law, but out of love. By so doing, **the tithe is perfected in our experience.**

God owns all we have - we are redeemed by Him, purchased by Him. Our tithe is the start of our love, our appreciation of giving back to Him, honouring Him, and thanking Him for what He has done.

God said it is more blessed to give than to receive. Check up on yourself. See if you are living by this principle.

> *"Give, and it shall be given unto you; good measure, pressed down, and shaken together, and running over, shall men give into your bosom. For the same measure that ye mete withal it shall be measured to you again."* Luke 6:38.

The principle is this: If we want to receive, we must first prime the pump. This means, a pump in order to pump water out of a reservoir to where it is needed- first has to be filled with water (this is priming). When the pump and line is filled with water and then turned on, the water is pumped out, causing a suction, which then draws water from the reservoir, causing a continuous flow. Our tithes prime the pump, and our offerings cause a continuous flow back from the reservoir of heaven. If we want to receive, we must give.

But even if we weren't going to ever get anything back, it should be a joy for us to give, if it means that through our giving the work of the ministry will expand, and others will be given a chance to know Jesus.

However, it is God's will to bless and prosper you. He tells us in 2 John 3 that His great desire for our lives is that we prosper and be in health, even as our soul prospers. He wants you and your family to enjoy His ultimate best in life. Experiencing His abundance that He provided for you by the sacrifice of His Son, Jesus Christ at Calvary, in order for you to have 'The Blessing of Abraham." (God's abundant life).

> "Be not deceived; God is not mocked: for whatsoever a man soweth, that shall he also reap." Galatians 6:7.

> "Cast thy bread upon the waters: for thou shalt find it after many days." Ecclesiastes 11:1.

GIVING AND RECEIVING REVISION

1. In your own words, give a brief summary of why it is important to tithe.

   ....

   ....

   ....

2. Why was Solomon one of the wisest and wealthiest men who ever lived?

   ....

   ....

3. Write out and memorize Proverbs 3:9.

   ....

   ....

4. Paul called giving a ....

   ....

5. List a very important tithing scripture:

....

6. Why do we give tithes and offerings?

....

....

7. According to the Law of Genesis Chapter 1, Every seed bears fruit after its own?   *True or False*

8. Write out and memorize Philippians 4:19.

....

....

....

9. It is the will of God for you to prosper.   *True or False*

   Back up the answer with a scripture ....

10. Abraham paid tithes to ....

11. Jesus Christ was a tither and we are told to follow His example.   *True or False*

N.B. Remember to break the curse of poverty off your life through the shed blood and powerful name of the Lord Jesus Christ. Remind Satan and the spirit of lack that they have no more power over your life. You are redeemed and you are now a new creation in Christ. You have been set free to win, set free to receive God's abundance through 'The Blessing of Abraham.'

The measure that you use to give, will be measured back to you and you will live in God's absolute provision and abundant blessing.

Chapter Sixteen

THE IMPORTANCE OF FELLOWSHIP AND THE LOCAL CHURCH

God made places before He made people, then God put the people in the places that He made for them. When God made Adam and Eve, He placed them in a garden, a garden that He had made. A place where they could grow, serve Him, enjoy fellowship with each other and fellowship with God.

God has a wonderful place in life for you. He has a plan and a purpose for your life. God has placed Shepherds, Pastors and Leaders over local ministries where He has given mission and vision.

We as God's people and God's sheep need to be led by the Holy Spirit, not our own emotions, feelings or opinions of others. Changing local churches or assemblies is a serious matter, one not to be taken lightly. God wants us to be trees planted by rivers of water, in green pastures where his shepherds can nurture and feed us the sincere milk and meat of the word.

Once planted, we are in the best place to be utilised by God for His Kingdom business. Pot plants are easily picked up and moved or blown over by gusts of wind. Jesus wants us to be a tree, whose roots go deep into the Word and Spirit. So when the storms of this life come, we are rooted and grounded by love into a local body of believers where we can stand together. Sheep don't lead sheep. Shepherds lead sheep, and as such, God would have us foster a healthy relationship with Himself, our Pastor and fellow believers in the local assembly where He has placed or planted us to grow.

Those who are planted in God's house will flourish.

Psalm 92:13 says *"Those that be planted in the house of the Lord shall flourish in the courts of our God."*

Planted in the house equals flourishing in life and business.

In nature, trees that are carefully planted and cultivated produce more abundant and better fruit than those that grow wild.

Just as a properly planted, fertilized and cared for tree grows strong and produces good crops, so our lives, when planted in the right house -nurtured, watered and fed spiritually- will flourish. God wants us as Christian believers (disciples) to flourish, grow tall and produce abundant harvest or fruit. This happens when we are correctly positioned by the Holy Spirit, planted, fed and watered spiritually in the right local house or body.

John 15:8 says *"Herein is my Father glorified, that ye bear much fruit; so shall ye be my disciples."*

Jesus says that His Father gets the glory when we, as disciples of His, bear and produce much fruit. So then, bearing fruit proves we are disciples. A disciple is a disciplined follower of the Lord Jesus Christ.

Discipline means;
   train (someone) to obey rules or a code of behaviour, using punishment to correct disobedience.
"many parents have been afraid to discipline their children"
synonyms: train, drill, teach, school, coach, educate, regiment, indoctrinate; (Google Dictionary)

To be a disciple of the Lord Jesus Christ is to be a disciplined follower of Jesus Christ. There are temporal and also eternal consequences for not following the Word of God and its principles and precepts.

Isaiah 1:19 says, *"If ye be willing and obedient, ye shall eat the good of the land:"*

To flourish in the Hebrew means to prosper; it has to do with prosperity. God prospers those that plant their investments in the house of the Lord.

Get Plugged In

God wants you to plug in. Get connected in order for you to grow and discover your purpose in life. As you sow faithful service and stewardship into your local Church, you will find that you are part of something bigger than yourself, that God Himself has designed in order to bring the world to Himself. That, my friend, is the local Church, which is part of His great

Church, in the world today. This Church His Body began on the day of Pentecost, and continues down through the ages to this day.

There is a place and a space for everyone. God has a purpose and a wonderful plan for your life.

You are a somebody. God doesn't waste his time to make nobodies and you were made by God. You are one of a kind. The only one of you that God has. You are special, and wonderfully and fearfully made.

The word of God tells us in, Matthew 18:30, *"Where two or three meet together in His name, there He is in the midst of us."* We are assured here in scripture that as we assemble together in His name, Christ is present.

We can see that assembling together is so important that God ensures us of His presence in a corporate sense when we do this.

Local Church

When we refer to the Church or the local Church as we will come to understand, we are not talking about buildings but about a living organism. A body of believers, called-out ones, joined by the Spirit of God to each other, who has the Lord Jesus Christ himself as their head.

The building then is the gathering place or sheep-pen where we gather, meet or assemble together. These gatherings or assemblies are for the purpose of worship, celebration, prayer, teaching or imparting vision etc. But the people are the real local church or body of believers in an area where God has placed, ordained and anointed leadership and oversight.

You are a Christian by the Spirit of God.

1 Corinthians 10:4 *"... And all drank the same spiritual drink. For they drank from the spiritual rock that followed them and that rock was Christ."*

The Called Out Ones

The value of the local Church has to return again to the believer. The word Church comes from the Greek word *'Ekklesia'*. In it's simplest definition *'Ekklesia'* means 'The Called-Out Ones'.

In Acts 7:38 Stephen refers to the Church of Israel as the *'Church in the wilderness.'* The Children of Israel were 'called out' of Egypt, which at that time represented bondage and slavery to them.

Called out of Bondage, **Called out of** Slavery
Called out of Debt, **Called out of** Fear
Called out of Oppression, **Called out of** Depression
Called out of Insufficiency, **Called out of** Sickness
Called out of Strife, **Called out of** Pain
Called out of Tyranny

But we are not just called out, we are called *out of,* to be called *into,* called into God. The bible says much about our new calling. Israel had one destination and that was to bring us to Christ and the Church, yes, and they were to reign and rule while doing it. The Church has one destination and that is the new Jerusalem, the city of God, in the new heavens and new earth. And yes, the Church is to reign and rule while doing it.

It's in the assembly of the believers under God-ordained Pastors and teachers that we learn about what we have been called into.

Once again, the building is the sheep-pen, the barn, a designated place where we gather or assemble to worship. We are the Assembly, the Church, the Called-Out Ones.

Not Forsaking

Hebrews 10:25, *"Not forsaking the assembling of yourselves together as is the habit of some"*

Here we read in the book of Hebrews that we are not to forsake. The word 'forsake' means to forgo, to give up, abandon, desert (e.g. a deserter from the army). Here we get an understanding of how important it is to fellowship or assemble together. God considers a person not meeting for regular fellowship with other Christians in the same place as a deserter from an army.

The word 'forsake' is a strong word. A Christian that is not attending fellowship where it is practically possible to do so, has abandoned their fellow Christians. Remember, we are in

God's army, God's body, God's family. Since you have been adopted into the family of God, a person that forsakes regular fellowship, orphans themselves from the rest of the family and the life and support that it gives.

We can see from the above scripture, (Hebrews 10:25) that some people have actually acquired a habit of forsaking fellowship and accountability to spiritual oversight, that God has placed in their lives, for their well-being and protection. There are habits that propel us to success, and other habits will bring us down. You need fellowship in order that you yourself can receive and learn from others. But you, as part of the body, have something that is precious, a gift from God, to give to others in order for them to learn and grow. We are not an island. We are a body of believers that need each other and the God-given gifts/ministries that He has placed in each one of us.

> Romans 12:6-8 says, *"Having then gifts differing according to the grace that is given to us, whether prophecy, let us prophesy according to the proportion of faith; Or ministry, let us wait on our ministering: or he that teacheth, on teaching; Or he that exhorteth, on exhortation: he that giveth, let him do it with simplicity; he that ruleth, with diligence; he that sheweth mercy, with cheerfulness."*

People do what they value and they value what they do. We must place a high value on local Church life and fellowship. Getting to know one another, connecting with other Christians for the purpose of encouraging each other, praying together, building each other up in the faith, are vital to our personal spiritual growth.

A Partnership Made in Heaven

"God has placed first in the Church apostles, prophets, evangelists, pastors and teachers, for the perfecting of the saints, for the work of the ministry, for the edifying of the body of Christ." Ephesians 4:11-12 (Additional reading Eph 4:1-32).

We can see from the above scripture that God has an established order within His Church. Pastors are a vital part of this established order. The word Pastor here also means Shepherd. The Pastor or Shepherd, according to the Biblical meaning, is the feeder, protector and ruler of a flock of people. Someone whom the Lord raises up to be the total carer of His flock. As we look at the language used in the Greek, we see God draws parallels and pictures to that of a Shepherd watching over and caring for His sheep. God is Himself the Chief Shepherd, and has raised up and placed in His Church or His body, pastor/shepherds under Him to have care, rule, oversight, protection and responsibility for His people/sheep.

It is vitally important that you have mentors and men and women of God in your life. God has placed the five-fold ministry in the Church, specifically to perfect His people for the work of the ministry. These leaders are to be encourager's, people who pray for us, teach us, and build us up in the faith. God has a specific plan and purpose for your life. These leaders play a vital part in helping us discover that plan and purpose. Every believer should be ministered to by this five-fold ministry in order to grow and become all that God has called them to be.

A hilarious illustration of the futility and lack of productivity that results from refusing to partner with others is illustrated in the following story taken from Dr John Maxwell's book, "Developing the Leader Within You."

> "People who are placed in leadership positions, but attempt to do it all alone, will someday come to the same conclusion as the brick layer who tried to move five hundred pounds of bricks from the top of a four-story building to the sidewalk below. His problem was that he tried to do it alone. On an insurance claim form, he explained what happened: "It would have taken too long to carry the bricks down by hand, so I decided to put them in a barrel and lower them by a pulley which I had fastened to the top of the building. After tying the rope securely at the ground level, I then went up to the top of the building. I fastened the rope around the barrel, loaded it with the bricks, and swung it out over the sidewalk for the descent.
>
> Then I went down to the side walk and untied the rope, holding it securely to guide the barrel down slowly. But since I weigh only one hundred and forty pounds, the five hundred-pound load jerked me from the ground so fast that I didn't have time to think of letting go of the rope. And as I passed between the second and third

floors, I met the barrel coming down. This accounts for the bruises and lacerations on my upper body.

I held tightly to the rope until I reached the top, where my hand become jammed in the pulley. This accounts for my broken thumb. At the same time, however, the barrel hit the sidewalk with a bang and the bottom fell out. With the weight of the bricks gone, the barrel weighed only about forty pounds. Thus, my one hundred forty-pound body began a swift descent, and I met the empty barrel coming up. This accounts for my broken ankle.

Slowed only slightly, I continued the descent and landed on the pile of bricks. This accounts for my sprained back and broken collarbone.

At this point, I lost my presence of mind completely and let go of the rope. And the empty barrel came crashing down on me. This accounts for my head injuries.

As for the last question on the form, 'What would you do if the same situation arose again?' please be advised that I am finished trying to do the job alone."

Your Pastor

Your Pastor is your man of God, called by God to shepherd and help you discover your calling in God. I believe that out of every ministry gift mentioned before, every believer should have someone, a man or a woman, called and appointed by God, to be their Pastor. Your Pastor will bring into your local Church/Sheepfold from time to time, apostles, prophets, evangelists and teachers. As you commit yourself to a true Shepherd, you will discover over time that shepherd will bring different ministry gifts into the church in certain seasons, as led by the Spirit of God to ensure ongoing growth and development of God's people.

Being part of a local church is absolutely essential to your ongoing personal development. You will grow as a believer into the person God has called you to be. You will come to discover how exciting it is to know your place within that body. Then as you begin to function from that place, in a local body of believers, together you achieve a vision or mandate given by God, to that particular part of His body.

I like to say 'Teamwork makes the dream work'. What you can't do by yourself, under the God-anointed and appointed leadership of a Senior Pastor and their team, then becomes possible. **Together everyone achieves more and makes a difference for the Kingdom of God.**

Your Pastor Needs You

Your Pastor needs you and you need your Pastor. God designed this unique relationship to be a partnership. The fruit of this relationship results in Glory to God and growth in your Church. God's vision and plan for reaching the entire world cannot be accomplished with just Pastors alone. When Jesus launched his ministry, even He, the Son of God, chose twelve men to help Him. Your Pastor cannot do it without the help of lay people like yourself.

God's plan is for you to be an integral part of the process of building His Church. God's vision for you is to make a difference in this world. Like your Pastor, you cannot make a lasting impact of eternal value alone, but in partnership, with the help of the Holy Spirit, there is nothing you and your Pastor cannot accomplish.

God has orchestrated that the local Church be the means by which we fulfil our potential. The Church, therefore, is the vehicle through which a Christian can make a difference in the world. In other words, the local Church is the ordained instrument of choice for world impact. You and I are the agents of that impact. The Pastor is the chosen leader of God to guide and coach the process.

God-Ordained Partnership

This God-ordained partnership with your Pastor is one of the most beneficial and fulfilling relationships you will ever experience. Your role in this partnership is vital. Your Pastor is required to be many things to many people which makes it difficult for him to know everyone in depth. You have a responsibility and a God-given desire and ability to know and understand your Pastor. As you come to understand this partnership, you will grow to respect, honour and appreciate this special gift God has placed in your life, to be a great blessing to you and your future. This will enable you to support your Pastor and local Church. Thereby you will find fulfilment and purpose in God's plan for your life.

Jeremiah 3:15 says, *"And I will give you pastors according to mine heart, which shall feed you with knowledge and understanding."*

Your Family Needs You

Now that you are born again, you are part of the family of God. As we have previously explained as a vital part of God's church, which is His body, you now have a part to play. Your family, the local church where God has planted you, needs you.

God has planted you in a local house, a body of believers, where you can grow. Now the gifts God has placed within you can begin to function in order to bring growth to that local assembly.

Ephesians 4: 4-7 says, *"There is one body and one Spirit, just as you were called in one hope of your calling; one Lord, one faith, one baptism; one God and Father of all, who is above all, and through all, and in you all. But to each one of us grace was given according to the measure of Christ's gift."*

We can see from the above scripture that you have been given grace, a divine gift of empowerment from God. You may not fully understand or know at this time what that gift of grace is, or how it is to be used to benefit the body. But as you grow under your Senior Pastor and five-fold ministry, you will come to understand and appreciate more your calling and place within the body of Christ, the family of God in the earth.

Ephesians 4:11-13 says, *"And He Himself gave some to be apostles, some prophets, some evangelists, and some pastors and teachers, for the equipping of the saints for the work of ministry, for the edifying of the body of Christ, till we all come to the unity of the faith and of the knowledge of the Son of God, to a perfect man, to the measure of the stature of the fullness of Christ."*

The Bible tells us that the whole body will grow and increase, when every person is bringing to that body the gift that they have been given by God. God will give you an anointing and unction to function, to bless and edify those around you, where God Himself has strategically placed you.

Ephesians 4:16 says, *"From whom the whole body, joined and knit together by what every joint supplies, according to the effective working by which every part does its share, causes growth of the body for the edifying of itself in love."* When people are out of fellowship, they are disjointed, like a limb out of joint. This causes pain and discomfort to the body. Both the body and the particular limb that is out of joint cannot function the way God intended it to function until that part is put back into place. (For further understanding, please read and study the whole of Ephesians Chapter 4).

Your Local Church Needs You

Your local church needs you and you need your local church or assembly, especially when it comes to giving. Bringing our tithes and offerings to the Lord, is brought through a local

Pastor and local assembly (Church). God has given your Senior Pastor a vision, a mandate to carry out for His Glory. God will call and add to that Senior Pastor, people who will get behind their Pastor and His vision in a financial way.

> The Bible tells us in the book of Hebrews 7:8, *"Here men that die receive tithes, but there He receives them who lives forever and ever."*

We can see from the above scripture that on this earth, God has appointed Senior Ministers to receive our tithes and financial gifts. But in heaven, at the same time we give to them, Jesus Himself receives them. We are in fact bringing our tithes to Jesus and giving our offerings to Him, by sowing into our local church.

> The Lord says in Mark 9:41, *"For whosoever shall give you a cup of water to drink in my name, because ye belong to Christ, verily I say unto you, he shall not lose his reward."*

You cannot even give a cup of water to a righteous man in the name of the Lord, and go without being rewarded!

God has placed a man of God in your life to receive tithes and offerings. A tithe is 10% of your income. An offering is a free will monetary gift in addition to your tithe that you give to the work of the Lord. God has instituted that through the ordinance of tithes and offerings, His work on earth gets funded.

> Malachi 3:10 says, *"Bring ye all the tithes into the storehouse, that there may be meat in mine house, and prove me now herewith, saith the LORD of hosts, if I will not open you the windows of heaven, and pour you out a blessing, that there shall not be room enough to receive it."*

When we all come together, we not only supply to the body the gifts God has given us, but in order for the body to grow, we contribute according to our ability financially as well. Most of the congregation works and receives different amounts of financial remuneration. The act of giving and tithing is also considered by God as an act of worship. We honour God through the act of tithing and giving, in order that there might be funds (meat, monetary resources) in the house of God. This is for the purpose of fulfilling God's great commission and spreading the message of the Gospel in the earth, while at the same time looking after and feeding our local ministers, shepherds and five-fold ministry. These can include missionary outreaches and evangelistic programs, feeding the poor, visiting prisoners, looking after widows and orphans. Basically, whatever God has specifically called your local assembly to do.

You will be empowered to prosper by giving to your local house.

> 2 Corinthians 8:9 says, *"For you know the grace of our Lord Jesus Christ, that though He was rich, yet for your sakes He became poor, that you through His poverty might become rich."*

2 Corinthians 9:6-12 says, *"But this I say: He who sows sparingly will also reap sparingly, and he who sows bountifully will also reap bountifully. So let each one give as he purposes in his heart, not grudgingly or of necessity; for God loves a cheerful giver. And God is able to make all grace abound toward you, that you, always having all sufficiency in all things, may have an abundance for every good work. As it is written:*

*"He has dispersed abroad,
He has given to the poor;
His righteousness endures forever."*

"Now may He who supplies seed to the sower, and bread for food, supply and multiply the seed you have sown and increased the fruits of your righteousness, while you are enriched in everything for all liberality, which causes thanksgiving through us to God. For the administration of this service not only supplies the needs of the saints, but also is abounding through many thanksgivings to God."

The Bible tells us where our treasure is our heart will be also. As we together combine our finances for the purpose of funding and extending the Kingdom of God, we not only get blessed by giving but we cause great joy and thanksgiving to God, from those that are recipients of the gift.

Matthew 6:21 says, *"For where your treasure is, there will your heart be also."*

Together Team work makes the Dream work! And the Bible says in Acts 20:35; *"It's more blessed to give than it is to receive."*

The Beginning

This is by no means an exhaustive teaching on the value, reason and purpose for being part of a local Church. It is just a taste and the beginning of an exciting journey of understanding, knowledge and purpose that God has for your life. Being a committed part of a local Church will bring a sense of great satisfaction, purpose and joy into your life.

You will find and make new friends who will love you, care for you and pray for you. You will discover a Pastor that God has specifically given to you, to help you along your journey of success in life. God desires you to win in life through Jesus Christ, and your local Church and Pastor are a vital part of obtaining and achieving this success that has been purchased for you at the cross of Calvary.

Christianity is a team sport, and your team needs you!

Deuteronomy 32:30a says, *"How should one chase a thousand, and two put ten thousand to flight.."*

Psalm 133 says, *"Behold, how good and how pleasant it is for brethren to dwell together in unity! It is like the precious ointment upon the head, that ran down upon the beard, even Aaron's beard: that went down to the skirts of his garments; As the dew of Hermon, and as the dew that descended upon the mountains of Zion: for there the LORD commanded the blessing, even life for evermore."*

Success is many things to many people. But one thing success is to all of us, and that is this, success is a journey, not a destination.

God has designed us, His people, to find success as a body: a team of believers who are making a difference by having a positive impact on their local community and their world.

I encourage you to learn and read more on the value and purpose of fellowship. One book I highly recommend, if you can obtain the copy of it, is "The Value of the Local Church" by Dr. John. A. Tetsola. (Please contact our ministry on how to obtain a copy.)

Proverbs 20:6 says, *"Most men will proclaim every one his own goodness: but a faithful man who can find?"*

Proverbs 28:20 says, *"A faithful man shall abound with blessings: but he that maketh haste to be rich shall not be innocent."*

2 Chronicles 16:9a says, *"For the eyes of the Lord run to and fro throughout the whole earth, to shew himself strong in the behalf of them whose heart is perfect toward him."*

God is looking for faithful people. Local Pastors are also looking for faithful people to be a part of their team, to do great things for the Kingdom.

Being a vital part of a local, thriving, growing assembly, is one of the most rewarding things you can do on this earth with your life. You will not only find fulfilment and reward in helping others and supporting your local pastors, but you will personally receive great satisfaction and rewards given back to you by God. Like the Bible says, a faithful person will abound with blessing. I dare you to join a local church and do something great with your life for God!

THE IMPORTANCE OF FELLOWSHIP & THE LOCAL CHURCH REVISION

1. Who or what is the local church?

....

2. What does the word 'Ekklesia' mean?

....

....

3. Write out the scripture Hebrews 10:25 & in your own words give a small understanding of this scripture.

....

....

....

4. Explain from scripture your understanding of the word 'Pastor' & their role in your life & spiritual development.

....

....

....

5. From Ephesians 4:11 write down the names of the five fold ministry gifts that God has placed first in the Church.

....

....

....

....

6. Explain the difference between the Church as the Body of Christ and what is commonly referred to as the Church building.

....

....

....

....

7. Write out and memorise Jeremiah 3:15.

....

....

....

8. Who was the Church in the Wilderness according to Acts 7:38.

....

....

....

9. In your own words and using at least two scriptures, explain the importance of tithing and sowing offerings into your local assembly.

....

....

....

....

10. In one or two paragraphs, summarize in your own words the importance of being planted into a local church. You can even include additional reasons why you believe it is important both to the Lord, other believers and yourself to be in fellowship in a local assembly.

....
....
....
....

Chapter Seventeen

JESUS WILL RETURN

The Bible tells us in the Book of Acts 1:11 that Jesus will come again. Jesus is coming back to establish a 1000 year reign of peace on the earth, known as the millennium. This will be after the seven year period of great holocausts referred to in the Bible as the tribulation (Matthew 24:29).

This seven year period will culminate or end with a great battle known as the Battle of Armageddon. At this battle, Jesus Christ and the returning armies of heaven will destroy the armies of the Antichrist and those that oppose Jesus Christ's kingdom.

The good news is that we do not have to be around for the seven years of tribulation.

> In the Book of 1 Thessalonians 4:16,17, it tells us, *"For the Lord Himself shall descend from heaven with a shout, with the voice of the archangel, and with the trump of God: and the dead in Christ shall rise first: Then we which are alive and remain shall be caught*

up together with them in the clouds, to meet the Lord in the air: and so shall we ever be with the Lord."

This *'catching up'* is referred to as *'The Rapture'*. The Word *'Rapture'* does not appear in the Bible, but the dictionary meaning of the word rapture is, to be caught up with great joy. In 1 Thessalonians 5:9 it tells us that God has not appointed His children to wrath, but to obtain salvation by our Lord Jesus Christ.

In Old Testament teachings, especially the book of Daniel, the last seven year period is called Daniel's Seventieth Week. It is a period made up of two halves, both three and a half years long. Jesus calls this time, the time of great tribulation, it will be worse than any other time in human history. It is a time of God's great judgement on planet earth for all of the sins, atrocities and evil that has been carried out down through the centuries against God and mankind.

It will literally be God pouring out His judgement on the earth and all of the powers of wickedness and evil on this planet. God does not want His children to go through this extremely terrible time.

Before the world enters this last seven year period, which in the Book of Matthew Chapter 24, are described as terrible years of wars, famines, earthquakes, pestilences etc., Jesus will come in the clouds of the air and catch His church, that is those who are born again, His followers, away.

Luke 21:36, *"Watch ye therefore, and pray always, that ye may be accounted worthy to escape all these things that shall come to pass, and to stand before the Son of man."*

The word here 'escape' in the Greek breakdown, means to vanish away from, to flee out of.

Jesus has promised that He will come back at His second coming to usher in His one thousand year millennial reign. I had a good friend by the name of Marvin Ford. He had died, and at that time, his Pastor (David Wilkinson) went into his hospital room, prayed for him and he was raised from the dead. Marvin shared with me, that during his time in heaven, he met Jesus who told him his ministry was not finished and he would have to go back to finish his course!

Jesus gave him an assignment to inform people about His second coming that would follow the time of great tribulation. He told Marvin that before He comes with His church at the second coming, He is coming for His church at the rapture. But before He comes for His church, He is coming to His church in great healing signs, power and glory.

The church before this seven years of great tribulation, will vanish away from the earth. And like Jesus was in the Book of Acts 1: 9 &10, the born again believers will be caught up to heaven, where we will live for seven years, until we return with our Lord Jesus Christ to enter into His millennial reign on this earth.

In the book of 1 Thessalonians 5:1-3 Paul writes,
> "But of the times and the seasons, brethren, you have no need that I write unto you. For yourselves know perfectly that the day of the Lord so cometh as a thief in the night. For when they shall say, Peace and safety; then sudden destruction cometh upon them, as travail upon a woman with child; and they shall not escape."

Jesus speaks about a time, that he refers to as the beginning of sorrows.

Matthew 24:8 tells us, *"All these are the beginning of sorrows."*

The beginning of sorrows is likened through the word of God, as a woman in travail about to give birth. It is birth pains! The closer the woman gets to the hour of birth, the more intense the pains and the closer the contractions.

I believe that right now we are in a time of the beginning of sorrows, at the end of the dispensation of 'Grace'. The world is about to enter the time of 'Tribulation'. At the end of this time, Jesus will fulfil His word and He will return to take control of the earth as Lord of Lords and King of Kings.

Be Rapture Ready

Matthew 24:44 tells us, *"Therefore, be ye also ready, for in such an hour as ye think not the Son of man cometh."*

1 Corinthians 15:51&52 also speaks of this mystery (rapture):

> *"Behold, I shew you a mystery; We shall not all sleep, but we shall all be changed, In a moment, in the twinkling of an eye, at the last trump: for the trumpet shall sound, and the dead shall be raised incorruptible, and we shall be changed."*

Jesus promised us in the Book of John 14 that He would come back for us, in verses 1-3: *"Let not your heart be troubled: ye believe in God, believe also in Me. In My Father's house are many mansions: if it were not so, I would have told you. I go to prepare a place for you. And if I go and prepare a place for you, I will come again and receive you unto Myself; that where I am there ye may be also."*

We can see from the current uncertain times we are living in, that the days before the return of our Lord Jesus Christ are drawing to a close. We are very close to the return of our Lord Jesus Christ.

> Romans 8:21-22 tells us, *"Because creation itself also shall be delivered from the bondage of corruption into the glorious liberty of the children of God. For we know that the whole creation groaneth and travaileth in pain together until now."*

As we draw closer to the end of the beginning of sorrows and the start of the great tribulation, the trials, tribulations, pandemics, earthquakes, natural disasters, sicknesses, mental health issues, wars and different types of wars causing heartache, famine and loss etc., will increase in magnitude and severity. They will get closer and closer together, affecting the entire earth. Great fear will be released upon the nations and the hearts and minds of people. Political leaders and governments will be in a quandary, mentally at a loss, not knowing what to do.

Recently a Pastor friend of mine asked me about the Return of Christ and the Rapture of the Church and what we can do to be ready when Jesus returns. Remember, Jesus told us to be like the five wise virgins that had oil in their lamp so that they could go into the safe place with Him (this I believe refers to the rapture).

> Matthew 25:6:10 says, *"At midnight the cry rang out: 'Here's the bridegroom! Come out to meet him!' Then all the virgins woke up and trimmed their lamps. The foolish ones said to the wise, 'Give us some of your oil; our lamps are going out.' "'No,' they replied, 'there may not be enough for both us and you. Instead, go to those who sell oil and buy some for yourselves.' "But while they were on their way to buy the oil, the bridegroom arrived. The virgins who were ready went in with him to the wedding banquet. And the door was shut."*

The Rapture is a Type of the Ark

Here is what I shared with my friend. The rapture is a type of ark. In the Old Testament, God instructed Noah to build an ark. This Ark was to save mankind and the animals from the impending judgement of God. This judgement was coming because of the rampant spread of wickedness, sin and evil deeds that people were doing before God and to each other.

Jesus said, *"As in the days of Noah, so shall it be in the days before I return."*

Noah was a preacher of righteousness and he warned people that God's judgement was coming and they should repent and prepare for it. There was a chance, an open door in the ark for people to enter before judgement fell. God gave everyone a chance to be saved.

Right now, God is giving everybody a chance to repent and be saved, ready to go in the rapture or the catching away of the church before God's judgement falls. I see the preparation time and building of the ark, as a type of beginning of sorrows that Jesus spoke of, before the judgement falls and a new day is born.

During this time, we must return to our first love. Make sure we are doing our best to win souls and prepare them for the rapture and the second coming of the Lord.

As previously stated in Luke 21:36, Jesus instructs us to watch and pray. We are to discern the times and seasons and not be ignorant or have our heads buried in the sand. We only have to look around, watch the news and we can see what is going on. We are then to pray, lifting up our eyes and staying in fellowship with our Lord Jesus and God our Father, through prayer.

As the Holy Spirit convicts and leads, we are to forsake and repent of our sins. We can do this regularly by taking communion with the Lord. Please read the last chapter on communion, in this book.

Kenneth Hagin would say, "Faith begins where the will of God is known." We must know that it is God's will to deliver us and keep us safe from the time of His great judgement and the wroth to come.

Raptured by Faith

Every promise of God is received into our lives by faith. Through faith, we receive the blessings of the Lord. Salvation is received by grace through faith. It is a gift of God. We receive healing by faith in the work of the grace of our Lord Jesus Christ at the cross. I believe, we receive salvation, healing, baptism of the Spirit, financial breakthrough and every other gift from God by faith. In the same way, we get raptured by faith. We must believe in it to participate in it! As Jesus said, "We watch and stay in prayer that we be accounted worthy to escape away from all that is coming on the earth and to stand before the Son of Man." Remember, Abraham's faith was accounted to him as righteousness.

> Hebrews 11:5-6 says, *"By faith Enoch was taken from this life, so that he did not experience death:*

> "He could not be found, because God had taken him away." For before he was taken, he had this testimony that he pleased God. And without faith, it is impossible to please God, because anyone who comes to him must believe that he is and that he is a rewarder those who diligently seek him."

Here we can see Enoch was raptured by faith because he pleased God. Let's do those things that are pleasing to God. Let us love God with all of our heart and love each other as we love ourselves.

Let's be vigilant and discerning in these times, as Jesus said, "Watching and praying." Let's continue to grow through life by constantly staying in communion with God, keeping our lamps filled with the Holy Spirit oil and the Word of God, waiting for that great day when Jesus comes to catch us away.

Faith pleases God, so let us have faith in all the promises of God. God is a rewarder of those who diligently seek Him. God wants to deliver you and your family from the judgement and the great tribulation to come, just like He delivered Noah and his family, from the judgement at that time.

Keep Your Eyes Open

> Hebrews 9:28 says, "So Christ was once offered to bear the sins of many; and unto them that look for Him shall He appear the second time without sin unto salvation."

Revelation 22:20: *"He which testifieth these things saith, 'Surely I come quickly. Amen.' Even so, come, Lord Jesus."*

JESUS WILL RETURN REVISION

1. What is meant by the Word Rapture?

   ....

2. When will the Rapture of the Church take place?

   ....

   ....

3. How long is the time of the great tribulation?

   ....

4. How long is the millennium reign of Christ?

   ....

5. List a scripture that backs up the teaching of the Rapture of the church. Write out and memorise.

   ....

   ....

6. When will the millennium begin?

   ....

   ....

7. Read Luke 21:36. From a Strong's Concordance write down the meaning of the word 'escape' (Greek meaning).

   ....

   ....

8. The battle at the end of the Tribulation period or seven last years of great holocausts is called what? The Battle of

   ....

Chapter Eighteen

COMMUNION

1 Corinthians 10:16, *"The cup of blessing which we bless, is it not the communion of the blood of Christ? The bread which we break, is it not the communion of the body of Christ?"*

Communion is one of the most powerful Christian sacraments that imparts divine grace to our lives. The word in the Greek is the word 'Koinonia' which means partnership and participation. Through communion, God partners with us in life. He participates in our affairs. Through communion, we become co-labourers together with God, and he becomes co-labourers together with us.

Communion is all about remembering Jesus, how He partook of our sins, becoming sin for us and taking our sicknesses in His own body as He died for us on the Cross of Calvary. Jesus became sin for us, partook of this so that we could partake of His righteousness, being made righteousness because He became or was made sin. Jesus took the full curse of the law that was due us for our sins and rebellion against God.

His blood was shed to cleanse us and to make the way for us to enter into covenant with God. This covenant we have with God is a blood covenant. It is sealed with God's blood, divine blood, innocent and holy blood. Through this blood (Christ shed blood) we enter into, and have access to, the full covenant of Abraham and all its blessings.

When you go to court, the judge will ask you how do you plead, guilty or not guilty? When we stand before our great God and Satan is there as a prosecuting attorney, and God asks us, "How do you plead?", we can say, "I am guilty Your Honour, but I plead the blood and through that blood and in the name of Jesus, I claim the Abrahamic covenant, the blessings of Abraham are mine."

It is the blood of Jesus that washes away all my sins. We are cleansed, forgiven and free, through this blood. We are a new creation in Christ, old things have passed away, and all things have become new.

> *"Therefore, if anyone is in Christ, he is a new creation; old things have passed away; behold, all things have become new." (2 Corinthians 5:17).*

You are justified by faith, just if as you had never sinned because Jesus has paid the full price for your redemption and freedom. We can now stand before God, holy and cleansed by the Blood of Jesus Christ, that was poured out for us at Calvary.

Through communion, we participate with God and all that He did on the Cross of Calvary in giving to us 'The Blessing of

Abraham' through Jesus Christ. We are then empowered for divine service in the Kingdom and ministry. We stand by faith in this grace in Jesus' mighty name. We remember Jesus, that it is now Christ in us the hope of glory.

This is the great exchange when we enter into covenant with God and we exchange what we have for what He has. We exchange our life for His. He gave His life for us. We exchange our sicknesses (He took them on the cross), for His health and healing. We exchange our sins (He took them on the cross, being made a curse for us) for His righteousness. We become the righteousness of God in Christ. (2 Corinthians 5:21)

We can now richly enjoy the full privileges of being a child of God. This is the Abrahamic Covenant Blessing and all that it represents.

> *"For you know the grace of our Lord Jesus Christ, that though He was rich, yet for your sakes He became poor, that you through His poverty might become rich."* (2 Corinthians 8:9)

Remember as He is, so are we in this world. (1 John 4:17b)

Communion should not be taken lightly, as to do so has serious spiritual and physical consequences.

The bible tells us, God remembers Abraham (Genesis 19:29), and it instructs us to remember Christ (Luke 22:19).

Communion, as stated, is remembering Jesus and all He did on the cross and during His earthly life for us. Before you partake, make sure you are not in envy or strife. Don't do it as a mere religious ritual or to commemorate a mere historical fact.

Not drunk or being in greed or unnecessary excessiveness. Don't take it irreverently towards God or His church.

Don't despise the poor and needy. Don't take it in unbelief, not appreciating the true significance.

We must properly discern the Lord's body, His shed blood. We must honour our brother and sisters in the body of Christ.

We must apply by faith all the benefits that are available to us through Jesus's body and blood.

We are to remember Christ's sacrifice and all that means for us.

By His Stripes, We Are Healed

He was bruised for our transgressions and wounded for our iniquities. Unsaved people should not take it without acknowledging their need for Christ and forgiveness, repenting of their sins and forsaking them. We must allow God to speak, correct and disciple us. To chasten (discipline) us where necessary.

The Lord's Supper

1 Corinthians 11:17-34 -

"Now in this that I declare unto you I praise you not, that you come together not for the better, but for the worse. For first of all, when you come together in the church, I hear that there be divisions among you: and I partly believe it. For there must be also heresies among you, that they which are approved may be made manifest among you. When ye come together therefore into one place, this is not to eat the Lord's supper. For in eating every one takes before other his own supper: and one is hungry, and another is drunken. What? Have you not houses to eat and to drink in? or despise you the church of God, and shame them that have not? What shall I say to you? shall I praise you or not. For I have received of the Lord that which also I delivered unto you, that the Lord Jesus the same night in which He was betrayed took bread: And when He had given thanks, He brake it, and said, Take eat: this is My body, which is broken for you: this do in remembrance of me. After the same manner also He took the cup, when He had supped, saying, This cup is the new testament in My blood: this do ye, as oft as ye drink it, in remembrance of Me.

For as often as ye eat this bread, and drink this cup, ye do shew the Lord's death till He come. Wherefore whosoever shall eat this bread, and drink this cup of the Lord, unworthily, shall be guilty of the body and blood of the Lord. But let a man examine himself, and so let him eat of that bread, and drink of that cup. For he that eateth and drinketh unworthily, eateth and drinketh damnation to himself, not discerning the Lord's body. For this cause many are weak and sickly among you, and many sleep. For if we would judge ourselves, we should not be judged. But when we are judged, we are chastened of the Lord, that we should not be condemned with the world. Wherefore, my brethren, when ye come together to eat, tarry one for another. And if any one hunger, let them eat at home: that you come not together unto condemnation. And the rest will I set in order when I come."

In the early church, they had social meals (love feasts).

2 Peter 2:13 *"And shall receive the reward of unrighteousness, as they that count it pleasure to riot in the day time. Spots they are and blemishes, sporting themselves with their own deceivings while they feast with you."*

Jude 12: *"These are spots in your feasts of love, when they feast with you, feeding themselves without fear: clouds they are without water, carried about by winds; trees whose fruit withereth, without fruit, twice dead, plucked up by the roots:"*

These feasts were followed by the Lord's supper. According to the Greek custom each brought his own provisions, the rich would fare sumptuously, while the poor had very little to eat. They were making the church a place to be despised. The poor were being shamed by their conduct. Instead of putting the food on a common table and having a smörgåsbord style meal - so all could partake together - the rich were eating by themselves and the poor by themselves.

The rich despised the poor, and this led to the divisions and strife of 1 Corinthians 11: 18 & 19, and to the drunkenness and shame of verses 21 and 22. This was totally against the teachings of our Lord. He taught us to love and forgive, not to show favouritism or partiality over another. He taught us, there is neither male nor female, there is neither Jew nor Greek, there is neither bond nor free. Racism has no place in the body of Christ. We are all one in Him!

These actions disqualified them for the Lord's supper and brought on the sickness and death - verses 27 and 30. Paul was sharing a direct revelation he had received from Jesus in verse 23: *"For I have received of the Lord that which also I delivered unto you..."*

Jesus told Paul in verse 24 that the bread is a symbol of His body. As the bread is broken, so was His body broken, marred and striped for us.

> *"As many as were astonished at thee; His visage was so marred more than any man, and His form more than the sons of men:"* Isaiah 52:14

> "Surely He has borne our griefs, and carried our sorrows: yet we did esteem Him stricken, smitten of God, and afflicted. But he was wounded for our transgressions, He was bruised for our iniquities: the chastisement of our peace was upon Him; and with His stripes we are healed." Isaiah 53:4,5

> "Who His own self bare our sins in His own body on the tree, that we, being dead to sins, should live unto righteousness: by whose stripes you were healed." 1 Peter 2:24

Communion is a memorial of Jesus Christ and His great love and sacrifice for us. Jesus healed us and set us free from all the power of sin, Satan, the grave and the curse of the law. We are to do this until he returns, as a perpetual reminder of the victory we have in Him!

The cup is a symbol of His blood, which was shed for many for the remission of sins.

> Matthew 26:28, "For this is My blood of the new testament, which is shed for many for the remission of sins."

> Ephesians 1:7, "In whom we have redemption through His blood, the forgiveness of sins, according to the riches of His grace;"

Colossians 1:20, *"And having made peace through the blood of His cross, by Him to reconcile all things unto Himself; by Him, I say, whether they be things in earth, or things in heaven."*

Acts 20:28, *"Take heed therefore unto yourselves, and to all the flock, over the which the Holy Ghost has made you overseers, to feed the church of God, which He hath purchased with His own blood."*
Revelations 1:5, *"And from Jesus Christ, who is the faithful witness, and the first-begotten of the dead, and the prince of the kings of the earth. Unto Him that loved us, and washed us from our sins in His own blood."*

Revelations 5:9, *"And they sung a new song, saying, Thou art worthy to take the book, and to open the seals thereof: for thou wast slain, and hast redeemed us to God by the blood out of every kindred, and tongue, and people, and nation;"*

1 John 1:7, *"But if we walk in the light, as He is in the light, we have fellowship one with another, and the blood of Jesus Christ His Son cleanseth us from all sin."*

Jesus' blood was shed for us and His blood seals the new covenant, which is based upon better promises.

Hebrews 8:6, *"But now hath He obtained a more excellent ministry, by how much also He is the mediator of a better covenant, which was established upon better promises."*

Hebrews 9:15-22, *"And for this cause He is the mediator of the new testament, that by means of death, for the redemption of the transgressions that were under the first testament, they which are called might receive the promise of eternal inheritance. For where a testament is there must also of necessity be the death of the testator. For a testament is of force after men are dead: otherwise it is of no strength at all while the testator liveth. Whereupon neither the first testament was dedicated without blood. For when Moses had spoken every precept to all the people according to the law, he took the blood of calves and of goats, with water, and scarlet wool, and hyssop, and sprinkled both the book, and the people. Saying, This is the blood of the testament which God hath enjoined unto you. Moreover he sprinkled with blood both the tabernacle, and all the vessels of the ministry. And almost all things are by the law purged with blood: and without the shedding of blood is no remission."*

"As often" - daily, weekly, monthly or yearly? You can't make a law on how frequently or infrequently you take communion. There is no set time or amount of times we should take communion. It is up to us. It's what we decide, but as often as we decide to do it, let's remember it's showing forth, declaring the Lord's death. It is remembering all that Jesus did for us at Calvary. By faith, it is receiving all the promises of God that Jesus obtained for us when He died on that cross.

I believe we should partake of communion regularly, because 1 Corinthians 11:25 states that "<u>as often</u> (and the word 'often' implies this is something that happens frequently) as you do this, you do it in remembrance of Me."

Communion is Remembering Jesus

I believe that the Church needs this constant reminder of what Jesus has done for us at Calvary. In the midst of all the attacks, temptations and trials of our modern world, it is easy to forget the absolute victory we have in Christ. We need a fresh vision of the power and victory that has been made available to us, the Church, His body, through our Lord's mighty work on the cross. We need to be reminded that we are *"more than conquerors through Him who loved us."*

We can access this grace, by faith and live in this divine empowerment of the cross, enjoying all of the privileges of the Abrahamic covenant.

As we partake of communion on a regular basis, we are regularly (often) declaring the total victory of our Lord Jesus Christ over all sickness, sin and death, and by faith declaring that He, our Lord Jesus has set us free-spirit, soul and body. That through Him we are the seed of Abraham, and all Abraham's blessings are ours by faith in Jesus.

All relationships are made strong through constant fellowship, communication and demonstration of a mutual love for the other party. It is good then for the church to have this constant reminder of God's great love for us, and as we partake in faith, in the right attitude, it is good collectively as a congregation to show God we haven't forgotten He loves us; we haven't forgotten what it cost Him to redeem us and that we still love and appreciate Him very much.

Communion can also be taken in your life group or connect group, your prayer meeting, where two or three gathers in His name. You can take it as a married couple, or any time you meet together with a Christian group. I like to take it regularly in my quiet time with the Lord.

It is Possible to Partake of Communion in an Unworthy Manner

Paul warns us about this in 1 Corinthians 11:18, 19, 27-32. He tells us that taking communion in an unworthy manner has serious consequences. "For this cause many are weak and sickly among you, and many sleep" (1 Corinthians 11:30). Where it says here 'many sleep', this means they have prematurely died, gone home to be with Jesus in heaven. He encourages us in these verses to examine ourselves or judge ourselves, in order to properly prepare ourselves to partake of communion.

We do this through personally examining ourselves, our hearts and our motives. Even if a part of our body is sick or giving us trouble, then we can rebuke the spirit of infirmity, in Jesus name and command that area to be healed and line up with the promises of healing found in God's word (refer to the chapter on 'Healing' in this book).

The Word of God tells us in, 1 John 3:18-22,

> *"My little children, let us not love in word, neither in tongue; but in deed and in truth. And hereby we know that we are of the truth, and shall assure our hearts before him. For if our heart condemn us, God is greater than our heart, and knoweth all things. Beloved, if our heart condemn us not, then have we confidence toward God. And whatsoever we ask, we receive of him, because we keep his commandments, and do those things that are pleasing in his sight. And this is his commandment, That we should believe on the name of his Son Jesus Christ, and love one another, as he gave us commandment. And he that keepeth his commandments dwelleth in him, and he in him. And hereby we know that he abideth in us, by the Spirit which he hath given us."*

Communion Preparation

We need to lay aside the weights and sin that does so easily ensnare us. We can then run the race that is set before us with faith and joy. There is a great cloud of witnesses, angels, peoples, family, friends and saints that have gone before us, that are cheering us on. You are a champion in Jesus. You were born again to win and overcome (1 John 5:4-5).

I like to say, "When you're going through hell, don't quit, keep going." This is an adaption of Winston Churchill's famous saying during the Second World War; "Never, never, never give in."

We must run the race (our life's journey in Christ) that is set before us with patience, while keeping our eye on the prize, who is Jesus, the author and finisher of our faith. You have great rewards in the heavens waiting for you, but until that day when God calls us home, He wants to bless us with His abundant and blessed life, now. This we can do by being doers of the word of God, not hearers only. We can keep on studying His word to receive 'The Blessing of Abraham' by faith, and applying His promises to our life.

I encourage you to meditate the following verses of scripture, Hebrews 12:1-3,

> *"Wherefore seeing we also are compassed about with so great a cloud of witnesses, let us lay aside every weight, and the sin which doth so easily beset us, and let us run with patience the race that is set before us, Looking unto Jesus the author and finisher of our faith; who for the joy that was set before him endured the cross, despising the shame, and is set down at the right hand of the throne of God. For consider him that endured such contradiction of sinners against himself, lest ye be wearied and faint in your minds."*

I believe that apart from all of the different sins and temptations that we all face, (which can be different from person to person); the big one that is common to us all, is the sin of unbelief. Unbelief ensnares, or tries to ensnare (beset) all of us, at different times. Unbelief or a lack of faith tries to get us to doubt God's word by focusing on the problem or our failures, rather where our focus should be, and that is on Jesus and the promises in His word.

Unbelief, if it is allowed to reign and rule in our hearts and minds, will bring us to a place of defeat in life! Unbelief must be overcome and conquered by the Word of God, through meditation of His Word and declaring His promises by faith.

Champions focus on the winning posts; they focus on the goal, keeping their eyes on the prize lest they become distracted and turned aside or ensnared. The devil and his dark forces, endeavours to put wicked imaginations, doubts and feelings of inferiority in our mind to get us to doubt God's word, in order to deny us the performance or manifestation of it, in our lives.

You Were the Pearl of Great Price

You can see here that when Jesus endured the cross, the word tells us He did it for the Joy that was set before Him. I asked the Lord one day, "What was that joy?" The answer that I received was, "It was YOU. It was the people that I was dying for, that would receive me!"

The scripture in Matthew 13:45-46, where it talks about the pearl of great price; was then quickened to me by the Spirit of God.

"Again, the kingdom of heaven is like unto a merchant man, seeking goodly pearls: Who, when he had found

one pearl of great price, went and sold all that he had, and bought it."

I realized that we, the Christians, the ones Jesus died for, were the pearls of great price. He gave His all, to ransom us, purchase us back from the powers of darkness, Satan and the kingdom of hell. You and I were redeemed by the precious "Blood of the Lamb."

When Jesus went to the cross, you were on His mind. You were the joy that was set before Him. He endured the cross for your sake, that you might be healed, made whole and go free.

Communion is a Time of Joy

Communion is a time to celebrate Jesus and all He has done for us and is still doing for us by His word and Spirit. He ever lives to make intercession for us.

> *"Wherefore he is able also to save them to the uttermost that come unto God by him, seeing he ever liveth to make intercession for them. For such a High Priest was fitting for us, who is holy, harmless, undefiled, separate from sinners, and has become higher than the heavens;* (Hebrew 7:25-26).

It was customary of the Israelites to joyously sing Psalm 118 at every Passover. So this was the song that Jesus sang just before He was led to the cross to die for us. This Psalm contains the words, "This is the day that the Lord has made, I will rejoice and be glad in it." Even though He was on His way to the cross to die for the sins of the whole world and receive in His own body the full curse of the law, He kept the joy of spending eternity with you before His eyes and on His mind. He focused on you and I being set free.

Communion then needs to be a special moment, a time of personal reflection and meditation. We can re-focus and prioritize ourselves on what is really important in our lives, family and church. It is a time to repent if we are under the conviction of the Spirit, and we can deal with our sins and unbelief, laying them aside. Putting them under the blood of Jesus, that is casting them into the sea of God's forgetfulness. Free of sin and condemnation because of what Christ has achieved. We can forgive anyone that has wronged us in any way and ask forgiveness if necessary of others, realigning ourselves to the Kingdom of God and its priorities.

Examine One's Self

We can pray to the Holy Spirit that He would correct, train, and discipline and lead us into all the fullness of God. In that famous book 'The Art of War', the author Sun Tzu said, "Know your enemy and know yourself and you will not be at peril in one hundred battles."

This quote came to mind when I read Paul's words about judging and examining ourselves. God wants us to do this for our own blessing and advancement. Not to feel inferior but to know our weaknesses, then apply His strengths so that Satan, the enemy, doesn't gain the advantage over us.

In a nutshell, we could say that this is a self-examination to diagnose any possible areas of pain or problem where the enemy could attack. We do this in order to fortify ourselves to win in life, through Jesus Christ. It is definitely not for the purpose of self-hate, or to feel unworthy or pull ourselves down in any way. But rather to get to know ourselves, so that the forces of darkness cannot exploit or utilize our own weaknesses against us.

Satan, the devil, always seeks to gain an advantage over you so as to cause you to fall or fail. He endeavours to condemn you, make you feel bad or hopeless. He wants you to feel insecure, unrighteous and unworthy of all that Jesus accomplished on the cross for you.

Jesus tells us 2 Corinthians 10:4-5,

> *"(For the weapons of our warfare are not carnal, but mighty through God to the pulling down of strong holds;) Casting down imaginations, and every high thing that exalteth itself against the knowledge of God, and bringing into captivity every thought to the obedience of Christ;"*

Communion is a Time to Sing and Rejoice

Through communion, we can remember Jesus and pull down strongholds in our mind by the Spirit of God and bring our hearts and minds back to who we are in Christ and who Christ is in us. It is the Spirit who brings us back to the remembrance of Jesus and what we have access to in Him.

> *"Let us therefore come boldly unto the throne of grace, that we may obtain mercy, and find grace to help in time of need"* (Hebrews 4:16).

The Holy Spirit is our comforter, strengthener and our advocate. By His grace, divine empowerment, we need to line up our thinking with God's will and plan for our lives.

> *"For I know the thoughts that I think toward you, saith the Lord, thoughts of peace, and not of evil, to give you a hope and a future"* (Jeremiah 29:11).

Communion should be a time where we sing songs of joy, praise and love to our Lord, because He is good and His mercy endures forever.

God desires to train us, equip us, teach us, discipline and correct us, so we can be winners through life. I remember, my friend and mentor Drummond Thom, telling me one time, about a conversation he had with God. He was on his way home from a major and very successful healing campaign in southern India. Over 300,000 people had attended, and many healings had taken place.

On the plane, on the way home to the United States, he asked God for more power to do more for Him. Drummond said that the Lord spoke to him and said, "Drummond, in order to do that, I must give you a revelation of yourself. If you want more power, you are going to need to examine yourself and get to know yourself. You need a revelation of your own heart, life and motives."

Each person should examine himself to see if he is in the faith and decide his fitness to partake of the Lord's Supper before he does. We should all make sure that we have dealt with any and all of our own issues, like unforgiveness towards another person or doubt and unbelief. Taking communion is a good time to regularly bring our heart and life into line with God's Word. It gives us the opportunity on a regular basis to monitor our own life and attitude. How are we living our life in accordance with God's Word and other people? Are we obeying Jesus's commandment to love God with all of our heart and to love others as we love ourselves? It is better not to partake if you are not fit to do so. Yet you should not feel that you are unfit, if you know that you are born again and are living as you should be, according to the gospel (1 John 1:7). No one is perfect, or has it all together! That is why we need a Saviour. There is no Saviour like our Saviour; Who loves us and wants us to prosper in life, through His victory that He bought for us, by His death on the Cross of Calvary.

Communion then is a regular opportunity to repent before God, allowing Him to straighten out or correct us in our hearts, so as to get fit to partake and live a victorious life in Him. We can ask Him for His forgiveness, making a quality decision to live our life according to His precepts. We can then partake with a clear conscience, thanking Him for His forgiveness and the cleansing power of the blood to wash away all our wrongs, empowering us to live the Holy life, God has called us to. Remember, "the just shall live by faith." (Romans 1:17).

> Mark 11:25, *"And when you stand praying, if you hold anything against anyone, forgive them, so that your Father in heaven may forgive you your sins."*

Colossians 2:6-7 *"As ye have therefore received Christ Jesus the Lord, so walk ye in Him: rooted and built up in Him, and established in the faith, as ye have been taught, abounding therein with thanksgiving."*

Colossians 3:5-10 *"So put to death the sinful, earthly things lurking within you; sexual immorality, uncleanness, inordinate affection, evil desires, and covetousness, which is idolatry: For which things' sake the wrath of God cometh on the children of disobedience: In which ye also walked some time, when ye lived in them. But now ye also put off all these; anger, wrath, malice, blasphemy, filthy communication out of your mouth. Lie not one to another, seeing that ye have **put off** the old man with his deeds; And have **put on** the new man, which is renewed in knowledge after the image of him that created him."*

Romans 6:14-23 *"For sin shall not have dominion over you: for ye are not under the law, but under grace. What then? shall we sin, because we are not under the law, but under grace? God forbid. Know ye not, that to whom ye yield yourselves servants to obey, his servants ye are to whom ye obey; whether of sin unto death, or of obedience unto righteousness? But God be thanked, that you were the servants of sin, but you have obeyed from the heart that form of doctrine which was delivered you. Being then made free from sin, you became the servants of righteousness. I speak after the manner of men because of the infirmity of your flesh; for as ye have yielded your members servants to uncleanness and to iniquity unto iniquity; even so now yield your members servants to righteousness unto holiness. For when ye were the servants of sin, ye were free from righteousness. What fruit had ye then in those things whereof ye are not ashamed? for the end of those things is death.*

But not being made free from sin, and become servants to God, ye have your fruit unto holiness, and the end everlasting life. For the wages of sin is death; but the gift of God is eternal life through Jesus Christ our Lord."

Romans 8:1-13 *"There is therefore now no condemnation to them which are in Christ Jesus who walk not after the flesh, but after the spirit. For the Law of the Spirit of life in Christ Jesus hath made me free from the law of sin and death. For what the law could not do in that it was weak through the flesh, God sending His own Son in the likeness of sinful flesh, and for sin, condemned sin in the flesh; That the righteousness of the law might be fulfilled in us, who walk not after the flesh, but after the Spirit. For they that are after the flesh do mind the things of the flesh, but they that are after the Spirit the things of the Spirit. For to be* carnally minded is death; but to be spiritually minded is life and peace. Because the carnal mind is enmity against God; for it is not subject to the law of God, neither indeed can be. So then they that are in the flesh cannot please God. But ye are not in the flesh, but in the Spirit, if so be that the Spirit of God dwell in you. Now if any man have not the Spirit of Christ, he is none of His. And if Christ be in you, the body is dead because of sin; but the Spirit is life because of righteousness. But if the Spirit of Him raised up Jesus from the dead dwell in you, He that raised up Christ from the dead shall also quicken your mortal bodies by His Spirit that dwelleth in you. Therefore, brethren, we are debtors not to the flesh, to live after the flesh. For if ye live after the flesh, ye shall die: but if ye through the Spirit do mortify the deeds of the body, ye shall live."

Galatians 5:16-26 *"This I say then, Walk in the Spirit, and ye shall not fulfil the lust of the flesh. For the flesh lusteth against the Spirit, and Spirit against the flesh: and these are contrary the one to the other: so that ye cannot do the things that ye would. But if ye be led of the Spirit, ye are not under the law. Now the works of the flesh are manifest, which are these; adultery, fornication, uncleanness, lasciviousness, idolatry, witchcraft, hatred, variance, emulations, wrath, strife, seditions, heresies, envyings, murders,*

> drunkenness, revellings, and such like: of the which I tell you before, as I have also told you in times past, that they which do such things shall not inherit the kingdom of God. But the fruit of the Spirit is love, joy, peace, long-suffering, gentleness, goodness, faith, meekness, temperance: against such, there is no law. And they that are Christ's have crucified the flesh with its affections and lusts. If we live in the Spirit, let us also walk in the Spirit. Let us not become conceited, provoking and envying one another."

We must correctly discern the Lord's body. That is, really decide we have faith in the death of Christ and lay hold of the benefits provided by it, not turning to one side or the other.

It is the Lord's body one must discern. It is by His stripes we were and are healed (Isaiah 53:4-5; Matthew 8:17; 1 Peter 2:24). Remember also, that the Lord's body is your brothers and sisters in Christ. We must become *"other minded"*, by this I mean looking out for each other, serving one another, esteeming the other more highly than ourselves. Loving each other and praying for each other in the love of God.

If one does not want to be sickly and die prematurely, then let him have faith in the healing which was provided by Christ, as well as forgiveness and other blessings. Nothing will be impossible with such faith.

> *"The fear of the Lord is the beginning of knowledge: but fools despise wisdom, instruction, discipline and correction"* (Proverbs 1:7).

COMMUNION

"Come, ye children, hearken unto me: I will teach you the fear of the Lord. What man is he that desireth life, and loveth many days, that he may see good? Keep thy tongue from evil, and thy lips from telling lies. Depart from evil, and do good; seek peace, and pursue it. The eyes of the Lord are upon the righteous, and his ears are open unto their cry" (Psalm 34:11-15).

To fear God is to obey God, by being a doer of His Word.

If we will thus judge ourselves and have faith in the work of Christ on the cross, we shall not have to suffer or go without the benefits provided for us. If we do not do this, then we shall have to reap what we sow. If we judge any sin committed, ask forgiveness, and put it away, then we are not chastened by God. If we refuse to judge ourselves, then He judges by chastening. (1 Corinthians 11:31-32).

Let us have order at the Lord's Supper and in the house of God. Satisfy hunger at home, and do not come together in disorder and condemnation. (1 Corinthians 11: 33-34)

> Hebrews 4:1-2 *"Let us therefore fear, lest, a promise being left us of entering into His rest, any of you should seem to come short of it. For unto us was the gospel preached, as well as unto them; but the Word preached did not profit them, not being mixed with faith in them that heard it."*

We which have believed do enter into His rest. Jesus loves

us. He died for us. God has many great blessings in store for the believer - let's reach out in faith and receive from our Father the rich and full salvation.

If we sin as Christians and make mistakes, let's not remain in them. Confess them to our God, and the blood of Jesus will wash us whiter than snow (1 John 1:9). Forsake your sins, turn from them and follow God again.

The Joy of the Lord is Our Strength

God wants the believer's life to be full of joy and the Christian life to be lived in the strength of the Spirit. One important way of achieving this is to...

Always be:
- quick to repent
- quick to forgive
- quick to forget
- quick to get up and go and serve God again.

You must recognise that faith in the blood of Jesus is the key to your life.

The Blood declares us righteous and removes sin. (Romans 3:25)
The Blood justifies. (Romans 5:9)
The Blood redeems. (Ephesians 1:7)
The Blood cleanses. (1 John 1:7-9)
The Blood looses from sin. (Revelation 1:5)
Through the Blood and the High Priestly ministry

of Christ, we have eternal redemption. (Hebrews 9:11-12)
The Blood purges our conscience from dead works to serve the living God. (Hebrews 9:14)
The High Priest (Jesus), through His Blood, mediates a new covenant for us, removes transgression and gives us an eternal inheritance. (Hebrews 9:15)
The Blood gives us boldness to enter into God's Holy presence. (Hebrews 10:19)
The Blood makes us perfect. (Hebrews 13:20-21)
The Blood sanctifies. (1 Peter 1:2)

Through the High Priestly ministry of Jesus, these and more of God's graces are extended to us.

Hebrews 10:10-18:
Authority over the powers of darkness (verse 13)
Perfected forever (verse 14)
Writing His laws into our hearts (verse 16)
Remembering our sins no more (verse 17); and
The removal of sins (verse 18)

These truths should always be alive in our hearts.

We must also have faith in Jesus because He mediates the new covenant on our behalf (Hebrews 8:6). It is the blood of the everlasting covenant that makes this possible (Hebrews 13:20-21), and we should recognise and appropriate its power, by claiming these promises in Jesus Name. The covenant of Christ is very similar to the covenants of old, but its depth and the transformation it brings are far superior to all that transpired before (Hebrews 8:7).

It is because of who I am in Christ, seated with Him in Heavenly places, that I approach Him in faith (Ephesians 2:4-6). So daily, I come to God in repentance, but at the same time, I draw upon Christ to sustain me. It is only as His righteousness, His victory, His joy, His peace, His faith is birthed within, that true holiness can be established.

COMMUNION REVISION

1. What is communion?

   ....

   ....

   ....

2. The Cup is symbolic of ....

3. The Bread is a symbol of ....

4. Write out and memorize Isaiah 53:4 & 5.

   ....

   ....

   ....

5. How often should we partake of communion?

   ....

   ....

6. We should examine and judge ourselves before communion. Why?

   ....

   ....

   ....

7. We can partake of communion in an unworthy manner.
   True or False

8. If we partake of communion in an unworthy manner we eat and drink judgement onto ourselves.
   True or False

9. Due to this, some Christians are weak, sick and some have even died, gone home to be with Jesus.
   True or False

10. Write out and memorize 1 John 1:9.

    ....

    ....

A final word from the author...

This book is designed to empower you to win in life through Jesus Christ. I pray these teachings continue to be a great blessing to you and that you revisit them often as you journey and grow through life. Apply these truths to the circumstances you face and share them with others. Always remember, that the number one key to success in life is, *"Seeking First the Kingdom of God and His Righteousness"*, (Matthew 6:33). Together let us love more, win more, reach more and do more for Jesus, till He comes.

Footnotes

The following is a list of resources and sources, read and studied in the preparation of this book. Plus, further thankyous and acknowledgements to individuals who have had an impact on my life. Their thoughts, prayers and inspiration (some of which I have included in this work) have helped mould me, enlighten my thinking and inspired me to grow and touch this world for Christ.

King James Bible
Amplified Bible. Jointly published by Zondervan and The Lockman Foundation.
NIV Bible. Published by Zondervan in the United States and Hodder & Stoughton in the UK.
Strong's Concordance. Published by Thomas Nelson Publishers.
Dake Annotated Reference Bible. Published by Dake's Publishing Inc.
Bible Hub. biblehub.com
Google Dictionary
Dr. Steve Ryder, for asking me to prepare and write this book and for his mentorship.
Dr. Reg Klimionok, for his conversations and teaching on Christian studies and the reason for church and the importance of fellowship. Plus his mentorship over the years.
Drummond Thom (Late) for his mentorship and wealth of teaching materials, encouragement and believing in me. Drummond, you will never be forgotten.
Don Gossett (Late). Author of over 120 books, for his love, teaching and friendship over many years. Enjoy heavens rewards Don.
Peggy Seals (missionary), for bringing to our family home all those years ago, bible studies on faith and victory by that great pastor and teacher, Billy Joe Daugherty (Late).
Apostle John Tetsola, 'The Value of the Local Church.' Baruch Publishing, New York.
Chris Harvey, my good friend and peer in the ministry. Your insight on communion lifted my faith to a new level.
John Avanzini, for sharing the revelation, 'You are never really free until you are

debt free.'

Lester Sumrall, for having an opportunity to fellowship with this General of God.

The words of T. L. Osborne, 'Healing the Sick, a Living Classic'. Published by Harrison House.

FF Bosworth, 'Christ the Healer'. Published by Baker Publishing Group.

Kenneth Hagin, 'Redeemed from Poverty, Sickness and Death' & 'ABC's of Faith'. Published by Kenneth Hagin Ministries.

Kenneth Copeland, 'The Blessing of the Lord: Makes Rich and He Adds No Sorrow With It', and the hundreds of hours listening to his teaching cassettes. Published by Harrison House Inc.

Jerry Savelle, 'A Right Mental Attitude' & 'Victory and Success are Yours'. Published by Jerry Savelle Ministries.

Bob Yandian, 'Ephesians: A New Testament Commentary'. Published by Empowered Life.

John Maxwell, 'Developing the Leader Within You'. Published by HarperCollins Leadership.

Jim Kibler, my good friend, for his writings on faith, tithing and 'The Blessing'. Published by Jim Kibler. All available on Amazon.

Norvel Hayes, 'Laying Hands on the Sick'. And hundreds of hours of his cassette tapes.

Charles Capps, 'God's Creative Power' & 'The Tongue a Creative Force'. Published by Capps Publishing. Available on Charles Capps Ministries website.

Hilton Sutton, 'Revelation: God's Grand Finale'. Published by Harrison House Inc. Available through Thrift Books.

Oral Roberts, 'The Baptism of the Holy Spirit' and 'The Miracle of Seed Faith'. Published by Oral Roberts. Available through Amazon.com books

Marvin Ford, 'On The Other Side'. Published by Logos International. Available through Amazon.

Wallace D. Wattles, 'The Science of Getting Rich'. Published by Elizabeth Towne Company. Available through Amazon.

E. M. Bounds: 'E.M. Bounds on Prayer'. Published by Whitaker House.

E. W. Kenyon. I highly recommend his works. All his books have had a profound influence on my life. Available through Kenyon's Gospel Publishing Society.

ABOUT THE AUTHOR

Dr. Shaun Marler is the Senior Pastor and co-founder with his wife Kerrie of World Harvest Ministries, an international organisation based in Queensland, Australia, World Harvest Ministries is committed to carrying out the Great Commission of Jesus our Lord, in feeding the hungry, clothing the naked, visiting the widows and orphans in their affliction, and preaching the Good News to the poor.

World Harvest Ministries currently has programs in India where the poor and destitute are given free medical treatment, orphan homes where children are fed, accommodated and educated, a ministry to widows who have been abandoned by society and a program to feed people with leprosy.

A portion of the proceeds of the sale of this book goes towards this valuable work. Which is making a huge difference in the lives of others!

World Harvest Ministries
PO Box 90 BALD HILLS QLD 4036
AUSTRALIA
Phone: +61 7 3261 4555.
Email: general@whm.org.au
Web: www.whm.org.au

Facebook: facebook.com/worldharvestmin
Twitter: twitter.com/world_harvest
Youtube: youtube.com/worldharvestlife
Instagram: @i_harvest

www.ingramcontent.com/pod-product-compliance
Lightning Source LLC
Chambersburg PA
CBHW030253010526
44107CB00053B/1698